THE
CHARLES A. BRIGGS
HERESY TRIAL

THE CHARLES A. BRIGGS HERESY TRIAL

Prologue to Twentieth-century Liberal Protestantism

CARL E. HATCH

An Exposition-University Book

EXPOSITION PRESS   NEW YORK

EXPOSITION PRESS INC.

50 Jericho Turnpike   Jericho, New York 11753

FIRST EDITION

© 1969 by Carl E. Hatch. *All rights reserved, including the right of reproduction in whole or in part in any form except for short quotations in critical essays and reviews.* Manufactured in the United States of America.

LIBRARY OF CONGRESS CATALOG CARD NUMBER: 70-98955

EP 682-46995-5

Dedicated to
S.A.
K.S.H.
J.T.H.
R.A.M.
who made this book possible

Preface

On January 20, 1891, Charles A. Briggs delivered an inaugural address at Union Theological Seminary that became the opening shot of an intense theological controversy that was to last for three years. The address led to the heresy trial of Briggs. Like few events in the last half of the nineteenth century, the trial showed that theological higher criticism had made deep incursions into American thought as early as the conservative 1890s.

A purpose of this study is to use the first heresy trial of Briggs (1891) as a means of measuring public response in behalf of the accused professor in order to assess how widely German theology had spread in an era of presumed theological conservatism. Another purpose is to show that the 1890s constituted an "intellectual watershed" in American theology as it did in a number of other areas of thought.

C. E. H.

York College
York, Pennsylvania
September, 1969

Contents

	Preface	7
I	Briggs, the Higher Criticism and Nineteenth-century Intellectual Trends	13
II	Briggs and His Explosive Address	21
III	The Conservative Counterattack: The Immediate General Reaction	37
IV	The Conservative Counterattack: The Detroit General Assembly	43
V	The Immediate Aftermath of the Detroit General Assembly: 1891	67
VI	Official Reaction to the Detroit General Assembly: Summer–Fall, 1891	75
VII	The New York City Presbytery— Initial Proceedings in the Briggs Case: April, 1891	87
VIII	Why the New York Decision to Prosecute Briggs: May, 1891	97
IX	The Indictment Against Professor Briggs: October, 1891	115
X	Briggs's Trial Before the New York City Presbytery: November, 1891	123
XI	Epilogue and Summary	131
	Bibliography	133

THE
CHARLES A. BRIGGS
HERESY TRIAL

CHAPTER I

Briggs, the Higher Criticism and Nineteenth-century Intellectual Trends

The decade of the 1890s has been termed "The Watershed of American history."[1] To those who accept this designation, it is first of all an economic watershed. On one side lay the "Old World" of *laissez faire* as contrasted with the "New World" on the other with ever greater control of wealth in the public interest. The 1890s were also years of social transition, for they marked the divide between an agrarian and an urban society.

The last ten years of the nineteenth century were also a decade of intellectual ferment. Between the Panic of 1873 and the eruption of World War I came a world-wide intellectual revolution with an impact upon virtually all disciplines. Like the new political and social ideas, these novel intellectual concepts acted as acids eroding the foundations of many time-honored pre-1890 suppositions.

The salient intellectual assumptions of the "Old America" need only be noted. In every field of intellectual endeavor, ideas were considered absolute with no direct relationship to time, place, or the special needs of individuals or groups. Some even assumed that ideas existed apart from the material world.[2]

In general, men deduced that these eternal concepts were valid for all ages. In religion the enthroned abstractions were equated with the "laws of God"; in biology and psychology they were

---
[1] Henry Steele Commager, *The American Mind* (New Haven, 1950), p. 41. But see Henry F. May, *The End of American Innocence* (New York, 1959), Introduction and pp. 393-398. May argues that this historical divide came early in the second decade of the twentieth century.

[2] Eric F. Goldman, *Rendezvous with Destiny*, paperback ed. (New York, 1958), p. 70.

dogmatically linked with "objective fact"; in philosophy, law, politics, and economics they were closely associated with "natural laws." As Eric Goldman puts it, "Always they were unchallengeable Truth, an ideological chain protecting America as if it was with iron strength."[3]

This optimistic trust in absolute laws and values was profoundly disturbed by the intellectual upheaval occurring late in the Victorian age. In economics the German-trained Richard T. Ely returned to America to point out the absurdities of absolute economic laws and to urge the acceptance of a controlled system of national economy.[4] In sociology Lester F. Ward and Edward A. Ross, like Ely influenced by German scholarship, helped demolish the social implications of Herbert Spencer's postulate of the survival of the fittest.[5] The harsh suppositions of the British scholar were replaced with a blueprint calling for collective social and economic control.

A similar reversal of values occurred in anthropology. Franz Boas, also educated in Hohenzollern Germany, undermined the foundation of the cherished American dogma of the supremacy of the Anglo-Saxon race. His most influential publication, *The Mind of Primitive Man*,[6] narrowed the meaning of race to common descent. Boas flatly denied the existence of an Anglo-Saxon race and posited the corollary that no group of human beings is inherently superior or inferior to any other.

This same ferment spread to legal speculation and theory. Leading jurists, like Oliver Wendell Holmes, Jr., Roscoe Pound, and

---

[3] *Loc. cit.*

[4] See Richard T. Ely, *Ground Under Our Feet* (New York, 1938), *passim*. One of the best essays on Ely is Sidney Fine, "Richard T. Ely, Forerunner of Progressivism, 1880-1901," *Mississippi Valley Historical Review*, XXXVII (March, 1951), 500-624.

[5] Indispensable to an understanding of Ross is his *Seventy Years of It* (New York, 1936). Ward's classic works are *Dynamic Sociology*, 2 vols. (New York, 1883) and *Psychic Factors of Civilization* (Boston, 1906).

[6] Besides Boas's *Mind of Primitive Man* (New York, 1911), his *Anthropology and Modern Life* (New York, 1928) throws light on the ferment in anthropological studies at this time.

The Charles A. Briggs Heresy Trial

Louis D. Brandeis,[7] based law on a pragmatic substructure and combated the notion that law derived from superhuman origins. "Man was not made for the law," said Pound, "but rather the law for man."[8] Such a line of reasoning meant that each generation of judges and lawyers was at liberty to tailor the law to meet contemporary social and economic needs.

In all spheres of intellectual investigation, pioneer critics of the old order insisted that the concepts which had for so long buttressed conservative America be tested by results. If they were not utilitarian, then they must be replaced by ideas that could meet that test. Wherever the measure of usefulness was applied, the outcome was usually the same: the neat and orderly Victorian universe was shaken. But if confusion and doubt replaced certitude and confidence, there was at least one compensation: the intellectual atmosphere was pervaded with the enthusiastic spirit of research, if not for ultimate truth, then at least for useful facts and empirical understanding.[9]

Theology, the intellectual bastion most invulnerable, also experienced a transformation.[10] Though Dwight L. Moody and Walter Rauschenbusch were contemporaries, their contrasting convictions illustrate the cleavage between the old and the new theology. One of the first effective evangelists to urban America, Moody held the Bible to be infallible and reasoned that this world was not worth saving. Professor Rauschenbusch, popularizer of the Social Gospel, entertained some doubts on the infallibility of the Scriptures, but he was strongly convinced that this world must be saved from

---

[7] Fred V. Cahill, Jr., *Judicial Legislation* (New York, 1952), is an able study on the history of legal theory. Samuel J. Konefsky's *The Legacy of Holmes and Brandeis* (New York, 1957) focuses on this period of transition. Roscoe Pound, "Legislation as a Social Function," *American Journal of Sociology*, XVIII (May, 1913), 755-758, is an excellent essay on how the theory behind law was changing.

[8] Pound, *op. cit.*

[9] Commager, *op. cit.*, p. 48.

[10] One of the most penetrating expositions on this subject is Arthur M. Schlesinger, "A Critical Period in American Religion, 1875-1900," *Proceedings of Massachusetts Historical Society*, Vol. LXIV (June, 1932).

social and economic inequities.[11] In contrast to Moody's otherworldly evangelism, Rauschenbusch wished to rectify social wrongs existing on this side of paradise. Rauschenbusch was representative of a rising generation of theologians determined to explain religion in pragmatic, relativistic terms.

Among the complex of factors that transformed American theology, three stand out as most important. They are biological evolution, higher criticism, and the study of comparative religion.[12]

The havoc that Darwin's theory played with traditional theology is so well known that it hardly needs description here.[13] However, very little has been written on the influence of higher criticism and the study of comparative religion on the "pragmatization" of American Protestant thought.[14]

Next to evolution, higher criticism helps explain why American theology was finally drawn into the mainstream of the global intellectual revolution of the late nineteenth century. For like Darwinism, higher criticism was based upon scientific investigation, inductive research, and a relative system of values.

Other comparisons can be drawn between Darwinism and biblical criticism. The two were introduced into America in somewhat the same fashion. The theory of evolution made its popular

---

[11] Goldman, *op. cit.*, pp. 83-84. Rauschenbusch's cardinal ideas can be found in *A Theology for the Social Gospel* (New York, 1917); but see also Vernon P. Bodein, *The Social Gospel of Walter Rauschenbusch* (New Haven, 1944), for added insights. Moody's viewpoints are to be found in Gamaliel Bradford, *D. L. Moody, A Worker in Souls* (New York, 1927).

[12] Merle Curti, *The Growth of American Thought*, 2nd ed. (New York, 1951), pp. 531-554.

[13] Darwinism, it is well known, made its effect felt in every area of American life. See Richard Hofstadter, *Social Darwinism in American Thought, 1860-1915* (Philadelphia, 1944), *passim*.

[14] To be sure, much has been written on higher criticism as a theological discipline. See Edwin A. Burtt, *Types of Religious Philosophy* (New York, 1939), pp. 308-318. But nothing comparable to Bert J. Loewenberg's studies on how Darwinism influenced America has been done in higher criticism. See Loewenberg's brilliant studies: "Controversy over Evolution in New England, 1859-1873," *New England Quarterly*, VIII (June, 1935), 232-257; Darwinism Comes to America, 1859-1900," *Mississippi Valley Historical Review*, XXVIII (December, 1941), 339-368.

debut with the publication of Darwin's *Origin of Species* in 1859. Its full impact, however, was not felt until after the Civil War, when Americans had turned their attention from fighting. The prolonged controversy that ensued reached its denouement sixty years later, when the world was treated to the spectacle of the Scopes trial.[15]

Higher criticism was in like manner formally introduced to America by means of a literary *pronunciamiento*. To be sure, Charles A. Briggs's inaugural address of 1891 was not a seminal work, as was Darwin's *Origin of Species*. It was rather a public proclamation that higher criticism had come to stay in America. Indeed, Briggs's inaugural was more than a manifesto: its highly militant tone made it a virtual call to arms to do battle with the "Traditionalists."[16]

Like Darwin's *Origin of Species,* Briggs's inaugural was at first rejected, only to be accepted eventually by the majority of Protestant intellectual leaders. Both Darwin and Briggs were ultimately vindicated by history.

Although there are striking similarities between these two harbingers of modernism, there are also differences. One is in regard to time. Evolution, though purveyed to Americans after 1859, did not reach the height of its impact until the Scopes trial in 1925. Higher criticism, on the other hand, which made its debut in 1891, reached its peak of intensity very shortly when in 1893 Briggs was condemned as a heretic.[17] This swift climax occurred because biblical criticism was a far greater threat to traditional Protestantism than was evolution. The "German science" not only threatened Genesis, it menaced the entire Bible. Hence the Briggs case provides a striking study of how conservative Protestantism in America

---

[15] William Warren Sweet, *The Story of Religion in America* (New York, 1950), p. 409.

[16] Charles Augustus Briggs, *The Authority of the Holy Scriptures: An Inaugural Address*, 2nd ed. (New York, 1891), pp. 41, 67.

[17] An excellent study of the history of the Presbyterian church since 1869 is Lefferts A. Loetscher, *The Broadening Church* (Philadelphia, 1954). Loetscher provides a good account of all three phases of the Briggs trial; see, pp. 48-62.

reacted to the encroachment of the new theology from the Continent.

A close study of the Briggs case is rewarding in another respect. It has been assumed that higher criticism never really penetrated America until it was brought to the public's notice by the censures of evangelist William A. Sunday. To be sure, Moody, sensitive to every threatening wind, knew that such a "science" existed. But he regarded it so lightly that he spoke of higher criticism less in anger than in sorrow: "What is the use of talking about two Isaiahs," he once asked, "when most people don't know there's one?"[18]

Evidence that after Moody, higher criticism was viewed as a somewhat greater danger was shown in the fears of evangelist Reuben A. Torrey. Successor to Moody, Torrey was so concerned about the rising challenge to the Bible that his meetings were often devoted to refuting the higher critics.[19]

Later, J. Wilbur Chapman, one of the greatest turn-of-the-century evangelists, demanded that all missionaries who doubted the inerrancy of the Scriptures be recalled from abroad at once. His most radical statement concerning the effects of liberal theology came in 1914. "The moral collapse of the German people," said Chapman when war broke out, "was the bitter fruit of destructive Biblical criticism."[20]

More than any other man, "Billy" Sunday symbolized the evangelical mind in this open war between "traditionalists" and "modernists." Whereas Chapman allotted only a portion of his time to refuting the arguments of doubt, Sunday devoted most of his sermonizing to denouncing the entire liberal trend in theology. Nothing inspired him more than to castigate all "those time-serving, hypocritical, hireling monsters" who had yielded their mothers' faith to the skepticism of the new learning.[21] When one liberal remonstrated with the evangelist for being so intolerant of evolution

---

[18] Quoted in William G. McLoughlin, Jr., *Modern Revivalism: Charles Grandison Finney to Billy Graham* (New York, 1959), p. 275.

[19] *Ibid.*, p. 366.

[20] *Ibid.*, p. 384.

[21] *Ibid*, p. 410.

and higher criticism, Sunday approached him the next night on the platform, shook his fist in his critic's face, and bellowed that the faultfinder should stand up with the atheists, higher critics, whoremongers, and adulterers and go to hell.[22]

By the 1920s higher criticism had become one of the chief foes of evangelical Christianity. The orthodox were greatly concerned that German theology had made deep inroads among the Protestant intelligentsia.

The Briggs case, like few events in that age, revealed that higher criticism had indeed made deep incursions into the American mind as early as President Cleveland's time. The remainder of this dissertation will attempt to explain, evaluate, and measure that impact by using as a medium of study the heresy trial of Charles Augustus Briggs in 1891.

---

[22] *Ibid.,* p. 411.

CHAPTER II

Briggs and His Explosive Address

The professor-theologian who has the leading role in this study was born in New York City on January 15, 1841, to Alson Tuthill and Sarah Mead Briggs.[1] The impressionable years of Charles Augustus Briggs were passed in the crisis-ridden decade which preceded the American Civil War. Despite the increasing sectional hostility, young Briggs decided to enter the University of Virginia.[2] This was an unusual choice at a time of acute North-South antagonisms. It doubtless demonstrates the peculiarly independent frame of mind that was always to characterize Briggs. There were, however, probably good reasons for the lad's political tolerance.[3]

By his junior year at Virginia, the New York student realized that the political crisis had deteriorated to the point of imminent civil war. Sensing the awkwardness of his position as a northerner in a southern university, he heeded reason and returned to New York City in 1861.

Secession of the lower South was quickly followed by fratricidal war. By midsummer the North and the South faced each other in

---

[1] Pamphlet in Scrapbook of Newspaper Clippings about the Trial of Dr. Briggs and Matters Pertaining to Union Theological Seminary, 1889-1893 (2 vols.), Vol. I, located at the library of Union Theological Seminary.

[2] Undated clipping from New York *Tribune* in Thomas S. Hastings (comp.), Scrapbook of Articles and Pieces Bearing on the Briggs Case, Collected and Mounted by President Thomas S. Hastings, 1891-1896 (10 vols.), I, 18. Hereafter cited as Hastings, Briggs Scrap Book.

[3] There was considerable pro-southern feeling in New York City among the merchants doing business with the Confederates. Briggs's charitable attitude towards the South can be partly explained by his father's belonging to this merchant class.

what proved to be the first of many bloody encounters—the first battle of Bull Run. Like countless other northern youngsters, Briggs responded to President Lincoln's call to arms. After having received little training, he was soon sent to Washington, where he joined other fledgling soldiers stationed at the capital to protect it from possible attack.[4]

For reasons not related, Briggs never completed his three-year stint. When the threat of immediate invasion subsided, the unseasoned warrior was relieved of military duty and permitted to return home to enter Union Theological Seminary. It was Charles Briggs's nature never to stay in one place too long, but precedent was broken at Union, and he remained there until his graduation in 1863.[5]

Thus, while most of his friends were getting a taste of one of the most brutal civil wars of modern history, Briggs was preparing for the ministry. But though theological studies kept him from battle, he was storing ammunition for a different kind of warfare to come. In 1891 he would spark an intellectual embroilment that would continue to his death in 1913.

After graduating from Union Seminary, the gaunt student of theology took a strange step. Instead of seeking ordination, he became a junior partner in his father's merchandising firm in New York City.[6] But he quickly discovered that he was no more inclined to be a businessman than a soldier. Bored with the mundane affairs of the market place, he decided to resume theological studies.

Following the example of many Americans who had preceded him, Briggs matriculated at a German university to complete his training.[7] The decision to go to the University of Berlin was doubt-

---

[4] Pamphlet in Scrapbook of Newspaper Clippings about the Trial of Dr. Briggs and Matters Pertaining to Union Theological Seminary, 1889-1893 (2 vols.), Vol. I, located at the library of Union Theological Seminary.

[5] *Ibid.*

[6] *Ibid.* See also Emilie Grace Briggs, *A Sketch of Dr. Charles A. Briggs* (n.p., 1899), pamphlet located at the library of Union Theological Seminary.

[7] Pamphlet in Scrapbook of Newspaper Clippings about the Trial of Dr. Briggs and Matters Pertaining to Union Theological Seminary, 1889-1893 (2 vols.), Vol. I, located at the library of Union Theological Seminary.

The Charles A. Briggs Heresy Trial

less a turning point in Briggs's life. To be sure, he had been introduced to the superficies of higher criticism at Union Theological Seminary,[8] but it was the influence of this world center of biblical scholarship that turned the New Yorker into a fiery apostle of German theology.

Letters from Briggs while at Berlin reveal a growing enthusiasm for the German critical approach to the Bible. In 1867, Briggs told a friend that he deeply admired the stimulating scholarship of his professor in higher criticism, Dr. A. I. Dorner.[9] In this letter he admitted he was favorably impressed not only by Dorner but also by other prominant German higher critics.[10] The young scholar doubtless raised eyebrows back home when he concluded by saying that while he did not look favorably upon the cold rationalism of the German higher critics, he was impressed with their methods and results.[11]

Briggs's correspondence makes it clear that his conversion to modern theology was complete before returning to America. In a letter to one of his former professors at Union, he compared American with German methods in theology and caustically remarked that the Americans were far behind the times.[12] He added he now knew that his mission in life was to return to America and modernize theological studies in his own country. This he would attempt to do by disseminating German critical methods through American seminaries. Letter after letter reiterated this sense of mission and the opinion that "the great fault with American theology is that it is too little critical."[13]

After completing studies in Germany, the twenty-eight-year old Briggs returned to New York and was in 1870 ordained a minister

---

[8] Charles Augustus Briggs, *The Authority of the Holy Scriptures: An Inaugural Address,* 2nd ed. (New York, 1891), pp. 19-20.

[9] Briggs to Dr. Henry Boynton Smith, January 24, 1867, in Emilie Grace Briggs (comp.), Record of Letters, Manuscripts, Notebooks, Sermons, and Clippings (12 vols.), III, 418. Hereafter cited as Emilie Grace Briggs, Letters.

[10] *Ibid.,* November 26, 1868, III, 467-470.
[11] *Ibid.,* January 24, 1867, III, 418.
[12] *Ibid.,* May 6, 1868, III, 461-465.
[13] *Ibid.*

of the Presbyterian church. He promptly accepted a small but promising parish in Roselle, New Jersey.[14]

Rev. Mr. Briggs tried hard to take the ministry seriously. But as he had feared, he found that his temperament and interests no more fitted him for church work than for military or business life. He had too many scholarly interests to be happy in a small-town pastorate where the intellectual dialogue frequently revolved about the hibiscuses of elderly spinsters.[15] Moreover, he found his congregation disinterested and unsympathetic to modern theological problems. At the same time, he realized that if higher criticism was to be popularized, Roselle was hardly the place to initiate a program. Thus the restless minister began looking for another platform from which he could more effectively herald the good news of German theology.

When an invitation came in 1874 to teach at Union Seminary, it was almost too good to be true. Briggs had not been forgotten at Union. He was remembered for his exceptional record,[16] and he had made an excellent academic showing in Berlin, particularly in Hebrew and cognate languages.[17] In addition, Briggs, who was aware of the necessity of academic politics as well as creative scholarship, had been careful to keep in touch with some of the senior professors at Union.[18] The New York seminary was thus fully informed of the brilliant progress that its graduate had made in Germany. Briggs was therefore not completely surprised when summoned to Union. The change was not only pleasant but challenging.

The former pastor's title at the seminary was Professor of Hebrew and Cognate Languages. Although Briggs found the new role incomparably more tolerable than the pastorate, he still felt

---

[14] E. G. Briggs, *A Sketch of Dr. Charles A. Briggs.*

[15] *Ibid.*

[16] See Emilie Grace Briggs, Letters, Vol. III, *passim*. The letters between Briggs and Dr. Henry Boynton Smith are especially informative as to Briggs's academic career at Union.

[17] Briggs to Dr. Henry Boynton Smith, May 6, 1868, *ibid.*, III, 461-465.

[18] *Ibid.*, Vol. III, *passim*. See especially letters exchanged between Briggs and Dr. Henry Boynton Smith.

hemmed in. The very nature of his subject matter did not offer the desired opportunity to purvey biblical criticism. Moreover, most of his time was consumed with helping students master the complexities of the Hebrew alphabet and grammar. He chafed under the realization that time was passing rapidly by and that he had not yet found the proper means to advertise the modern German approach to the Testaments. By 1890, he was inwardly burning with discontent. Other conditions at Union increased his ill humor. In 1870, Union entered into an agreement with the General Assembly of the Presbyterian Church under which the New York seminary became one of a number of Presbyterian seminaries. This arrangement had a direct bearing on Briggs's wish to propagate higher criticism: the official Presbyterian position was staunchly opposed to German theology.[19]

However, the Presbyterian church's control over Union was not complete. In contrast to other Presbyterian seminaries like Princeton and McCormick, Union retained much local autonomy as stipulated by the Compact of 1870.[20] In addition, Union had an unusually progressive faculty for an era marked by conservative theological beliefs. Most members of the faculty were either overt or covert sympathizers of the doctrines of Julius Wellhausen.[21] Even

---

[19] New York *Herald*, October 18, 1891; "The Storm Center At Detroit," New York *Evangelist*, June 4, 1891.

[20] Philip Schaff, "Other Heresy Trials and the Briggs Case," unmarked and undated article in Hastings, Briggs Scrap Book, III, 5-6.

[21] Julius Wellhausen (1844-1918) has rightly been called the "Father of Higher Criticism." Probably more than any other, he gave the higher criticism movement its great impetus on the Continent. Wellhausen pioneered the historical method as applicable to the Old Testament. He concluded that the Pentateuch was written not by Moses according to the orthodox view but by four men, whom he referred to as J.E.P.D. The influence that Wellhausen had on American theologians is incalculable. Briggs's favorite teacher at the University of Berlin, A. I. Dorner, was a Wellhausen disciple. See Isadore Singer, *et al.* (editors), *The Jewish Encyclopedia*, 12 vols. (New York, 1901-1906), XII, 500, for a good account of Wellhausen's life. See Briggs to Henry Boynton Smith, November 26, 1868, in Emilie Grace Briggs, Letters, III, 467-470, for an evaluation of the impact of German higher criticism upon American scholars in Germany during the nineteenth century.

the seminary's distinguished president, Thomas S. Hastings, was not entirely opposed to the insurgent theology.[22] Despite these advantages, Briggs realized that Union was still a Presbyterian school and that for this reason he had to tread cautiously. He was not, however, one to practice assiduously the virtue of one of his favorite Old Testament characters. Job's boils taught patience, but the torment to spread the "German gospel" precluded that the Union teacher would master that lesson.

Restrained in the classroom, Briggs allowed himself more freedom in publications. But even here the German-trained theologian was forced to circumspection because the Presbyterian church possessed the power to cancel his appointment at the seminary for heterodox publications as well as classroom lectures. Briggs was thus forced to discipline himself even in his writings; his books and pamphlets, accordingly, were studded with guarded qualifications.[23]

As it was increasingly obvious that Briggs was becoming more and more anxious to fulfill his mission,[24] his colleagues were not surprised to learn of academic maneuverings to create for him a new position which would allow greater opportunity to promulgate higher criticism. The stratagem was to persuade the executive board of the seminary to create a new department of higher criticism with Briggs as chairman. Wisely concluding that the repugnant term "higher criticism" would hurt his plan, Briggs suggested the euphemism "Department of Biblical Theology."[25]

---

[22] New York *Times,* October 29, 1891.

[23] "Dr. Briggs at Close Range," undated clipping from the New York *World* in Hastings, Briggs Scrap Book, I, 53-54. Briggs was not always circumspect. He had aroused enough attention by his writings that the secular as well as the religious press observed he was recognized as early as 1880 as a leading exponent of higher criticism in America; see the New York *Tribune,* October 5, 1891.

[24] Clipping of minutes and comments concerning the proceedings of the Detroit General Assembly (1891) in Hastings, Briggs Scrap Book, I, 22-23.

[25] Schaff, "Other Heresy Trials and the Briggs Case." Biblical theology as a discipline was altogether new; the four great divisions of theology at the turn of the century were (1) exegetical, (2) historical, (3) systematic, and (4) practical, in character. See Charles A. Briggs, "Theological Education and Its Needs," unmarked and undated pamphlet in Hastings, Briggs Scrap Book, III, 5.

The Charles A. Briggs Heresy Trial

The plan was fine in theory. To implement the blueprint, however, it was necessary not only to persuade the seminary's decision makers but to find subsidization for the venture.

As it turned out, little difficulty was encountered in winning over the administration, for Briggs had zealous sympathizers among the faculty. More important, he was highly regarded by the venerable chairman of the directorate, Charles Butler.[26]

Butler had known Briggs from boyhood and had for years held him in high esteem as friend and protégé; accordingly, the senior director was happy to assist his "spiritual son" in any way possible. The result was that the elderly gentleman promised to support the new department in discussions in the directorate.[27] In addition, he underwrote it financially.[28] Thus, on April 25, 1890, the seminary received $100,000 earmarked "solely for the support" of the chair in the new Department of Biblical Theology.[29] Butler's influence was such that his request was equivalent to a command. On November 11, 1890, the board unanimously accepted both Butler's bequest and his proposal that "Dr. Briggs . . . be the one to fill the Chair."[30] Only later was it learned that one of Butler's chief motives was his own interest in the modernization of American theology.[31]

In laying plans for ceremonies for the new department and chair, Briggs showed a reluctance to use the inaugural address to reveal his objectives. Discussing the matter with Butler, he suggested the neutral subject "The Geography of the Bible" as a good topic. Butler, old in body but young in mind, threw caution to the winds and counseled the younger man: "Just take the subject

---

[26] Undated clipping from the New York *Tribune* in Hastings, Briggs Scrap Book, I, 18.

[27] C. A. Briggs, *The Authority of the Holy Scriptures*, p. 1.

[28] *Ibid.*, p. 9.

[29] *Ibid.*

[30] *Ibid.*, p. 3. The chair was called the Edward Robinson Chair of Biblical Theology; see the pamphlet *The Edward Robinson Chair of Biblical Theology in the Union Theological Seminary, New York* (n.p., 1891), in the library of Union Theological Seminary.

[31] Undated clipping from the New York *Tribune* in Hastings, Briggs Scrap Book, I, 18.

that you have all along wanted to present and boldly give us your address upon that theme."[32]

An ominous quiet characterized the two months between Butler's recommendation to the board and Briggs's inaugural address. The professor's silence is partially explained by the fact that he was meticulously preparing the lecture for that unforgettable evening of January 20, 1891.

The calm was disturbed by a single rumble which warned of the storm soon to break. On January 7, Briggs wrote to the board gratefully accepting the nomination to the new chair. Containing the usual pleasantries, the letter offered hints of the inaugural theme. Briggs noted that the new chair would help him achieve a long-standing ambition, and he promised to push forward the work of the new department vigorously "because up until now Biblical scholars have been long held in bondage to ecclesiasticism and dogmatism."[33] He went on to say he wished to rid the accumulations of medieval dogmatisms with the scale of biblical criticism.[34] Some of the more conservative members of the board probably squirmed in their seats as Briggs's letter was read. However, best thoughts were allowed to prevail, and arrangements proceeded for the approaching evening of formalities.

The night of the inauguration came in the midst of a January snowstorm. Despite below-freezing weather, many of the city's dignitaries and their wives braved the wintry weather in anticipation of an evening of warm Christian fellowship. Adams Chapel at Union Seminary was soon filled to capacity by members of the board, visiting ministers, college professors, elders, eminent laymen, and curious students.[35]

Formalities began with devotions, followed by an announcement of the transfer of Dr. Briggs from the Department of Hebrew to the Department of Biblical Theology.[36] Then Professor Briggs

---

[32] Undated clipping from the *Presbyterian Faith* in Hastings, *ibid.*, I, 22-23.
[33] C. A. Briggs, *The Authority of the Holy Scriptures*, p. 4.
[34] *Ibid.*
[35] Unmarked and undated newspaper clipping in Hastings, Briggs Scrap Book, I, 2-3.
[36] C. A. Briggs, *The Authority of the Holy Scriptures*, p. 10.

The Charles A. Briggs Heresy Trial

was requested to submit to the pledge required of newly appointed or transferred teachers at all Presbyterian seminaries. This involved making a public declaration of belief in the Holy Scriptures as the only infallible rule of faith and practice.[37] Little did the unsuspecting assembly realize that in less than five minutes, all that had been professed would be repudiated.

Immediately before the inaugural address, fond memories were stirred momentarily as an old classmate of Briggs delivered the "charge." One wonders what thoughts must have been in the newly installed chairman's mind as his long-time friend piously intonated ". . . to remember that the Bible is the Book of God . . . and that we do not attempt to explain it . . . but accept it, believe in it, and hope in it."[38] With a touch of tragicomedy, the classmate concluded: ". . . and when your great work is finished, may His 'Well done' be pronounced upon His good and faithful servant."[39] Briggs's minister-friend might have been much more measured in his encomium if he had suspected the speaker of the evening was about to embark on a course that would prove him to be, in the eyes of the orthodox, a faithless minion of the Lord of Hosts.

Between the charge and the inaugural address, there was a momentary stir. A hush descended quickly as Briggs was invited to deliver the lecture of the evening. The professor moved slowly into his discourse. He prefaced his speech with a "response to the charge" which aroused curiosity as to what was to follow. Thanking all concerned for the honor bestowed on him,[40] Briggs eulogized the late Professor Edward Robinson, after whom the new chair was named. Robinson was praised for having been one who would not "endure sham of any kind . . . who was an explorer and

---

[37] *Ibid.*

[38] *Ibid.*, p. 14.

[39] *Ibid.*, p. 18.

[40] The two men most responsible for Briggs's new department were David McAlpin and Charles Butler, both friends and benefactors of the seminary. McAlpin's name is remembered well at Union even today; the McAlpin Rare Book Room at the Seminary is one of the richest manuscript depositories of its kind. All of Briggs's manuscripts are there.

builder . . . who was great because he had vigorously appreciated the best treasurers of German learning."[41]

At this point the new chairman straightened, grasped the lectern with both hands, and began his famous inaugural address in dead earnest. Briggs probably never suspected he was about to fire the opening shot of the battle over higher criticism in the United States.

The title of his lecture sounded innocuous enough: "The Authority of the Holy Scriptures." But here inoffensiveness began and ended.

Briggs immediately plunged into the substance of his lecture with the zeal of a reformer. "It seems to be my duty," he declared, "to set forth my views fully and frankly."[42] The next seventy minutes were a masterly exercise in adhering to that resolve.

He instantly set his Protestant audience on edge by asserting there were three, not one, great fountains of divine authority: the institutional church, reason, and the Bible.[43] He went on to declare that a striking illustration of one who had found God through the institutional church was the Roman Catholic convert Cardinal John H. Newman.[44] In the same manner, Briggs noted an illustration of another man who had found God solely through reason: the rationalist James Martineau.[45] He finally referred to Charles H. Spurgeon, famed English minister, as the most salient example of one who had discovered God exclusively through the Bible. Shocking an audience already discomforted, Briggs suggested, "May we not conclude that these three men are representative Christians of our time, and that each, in his own way, found God either through the Church, Reason, or the Bible?"[46] What seemed to nettle the Presbyterian listeners most was the implication that reason and the church were equal to the Bible as infallible moral guides to life.

---

[41] C. A. Briggs, *The Authority of the Holy Scriptures*, pp. 19-20.
[42] *Ibid.*, p. 23.
[43] *Ibid.*, p. 24.
[44] *Ibid.*, p. 25.
[45] *Ibid.*, p. 27.
[46] *Ibid.*, p. 28.

The Charles A. Briggs Heresy Trial 31

While these introductory remarks led the audience to believe that the new chairman doubted the Bible's monopoly on morality, subsequent declarations lent credence to the growing suspicion that the German-trained theologian was out to destroy belief in the infallibility of the Bible.

"But of all these three ways to God," said Briggs as he momentarily drew away from the lectern, "no one of these has been so obstructed as the Holy Bible."[47] He continued by noting that although the sixteenth-century Protestant reformers had been careful to place the Bible in true perspective, their successors had exalted the Scriptures beyond all common sense. The unthinking successors of Luther and Calvin had enveloped the Bible with protective creeds, conciliar decisions, and dogmatic interpretations.[48]

The intrepid Briggs seemed impervious to the audience's hostile reaction. With thumbs in vest pockets he exclaimed: "The whole trouble with the Bible today is that it has been treated as if it were a baby, to be wrapped in swaddling clothes, nursed, carefully guarded lest it should be injured by heretics and skeptics." The Bible of this day and age, he added, had been shut up in a fortress and surrounded by breastworks reminiscent of the castles of medieval warfare. "The one big trouble with the Bible today," he said, "is that no one could get at the Bible unless he forced his way through the parapets of traditional dogmatism and stormed the barriers of ecclesiasticism."[49] The net effect of this, he continued, was to shut out the light of God, to obstruct the life of God, and to fence in the Bible, thus rendering the Book useless.[50]

Briggs by now had reached the moment of decision. Had he so chosen, he could have veered in the direction of orthodoxy at this point. He had thus far been only vexing, not heretical. If he had taken the right and not the left path at this fork in the road, he probably would not have suffered the pains of subsequent indictment. For reasons that can only partly be explained, he took the road to the left. In doing so, he passed the point of no return. His

---
[47] *Ibid.*
[48] *Ibid.*, p. 29.
[49] *Ibid.*
[50] *Ibid.*, p. 30.

next remarks branded him an implacable foe of orthodox theology and an ardent devotee of higher criticism. Some men in history have determined their destiny with words; Briggs was one of those men.

The first "barrier" keeping people from the Bible was "superstition." "We are accustomed," Briggs said with apparent emotion, "to attach superstition to the Roman Catholic Mariolatry and the use of images, and pictures and other external things in worship. But superstition is not less superstition if it takes the form of Bibliolatry." With diminishing restraint, the speaker shocked the faithful by adding, "The Bible has no magical virtue in it, and there is no halo enclosing it. It will not stop a bullet any better than a Mass-book. It will not keep off evil spirits any better than a cross. It will not even guard a home from fire half as well as holy water. The Bible, as a book, is paper, print, and binding—nothing more."[51] At this point Briggs's students broke out in roaring applause.[52]

"The second barrier keeping men from the Bible," said the speaker, "is the dogma of verbal inspiration." His comments were extraordinarily incendiary because the doctrine of verbal inspiration was (and still is) one of the dearest tenets of evangelical Protestantism.[53] The professor must have suspected he would have to answer in the future for the darts about to be flung at the very heart of the Protestant faith. He said, "We find that there are errors in the Bible. There is nothing divine in the text—in its letters, words, or clauses. It is claimed by the Traditionalists that, though the English Bible as such is not verbally inspired, the Originals—the Hebrew Old Testament and Greek New Testament

---

[51] *Ibid.*

[52] Undated clipping from the New York *Tribune* in Hastings, Briggs Scrap Book, I, 2-3.

[53] Evangelical Protestantism holds that the Scriptures are God-inspired in the literal sense—not only the ideas but the very words of the Bible are God-given. The Traditionalists of Briggs's day were known later as Fundamentalists. For a good account of the Fundamentalists' view of inspiration, see Everett F. Harrison (editor), *Baker's Dictionary of Theology* (Grand Rapids, 1960), p. 286; also see Augustus H. Strong, *Systematic Theology* (Philadelphia, 1907), pp. 210-211.

The Charles A. Briggs Heresy Trial

—are inspired down to the very word." This Briggs categorically denied. "Language is rather only the dress of thought. The same thought in the Bible is dressed in many different literary styles, and the thought of one language is as authoritative as the other. The divine authority contained in the Scripture speaks as powerfully in English as in Greek, in Choctaw as in Aramaic, in Chinese as in Hebrew."[54] Again Briggs's students broke out in roisterous applause.[55]

Elated by this response, Briggs went on to the next point with greater abandon. There was, he maintained, still a third barrier to the Bible: this was the false notion that the Scripture was inerrant. Conceding that finding errors in the Bible was disconcerting, Briggs nevertheless insisted that "the Higher Criticism finds them, and we must meet the issue whether it destroys the authority of the Bible or not." Shifting from behind the lectern to the edge of the platform, he exclaimed: "I shall venture to affirm that there are errors in the Scriptures that no one has been able to explain away; and even the idea and theory that they were not in the original texts is sheer assumption! If such errors destroy the authority of the Bible, it is already destroyed for historians. Men cannot shut their eyes to truth and fact. The Bible itself nowhere makes the claim that it is inerrant. Nor do the creeds of the Church sanction such a theory. Indeed, the theory that the Bible is inerrant is the ghost of modern evangelicalism to frighten children."[56]

Adams Chapel was filled with angry silence. The thoughts of the orthodox were mirrored in the countenance of Dr. William G. T. Shedd, Professor of Systematic Theology at Union. Though he attempted to mask his feelings, Shedd's masquerade was a failure. It was obvious he could hardly contain himself.[57]

Briggs must have realized that his students' applause was more

---

[54] C. A. Briggs, *The Authority of the Holy Scriptures,* pp. 31-32.

[55] Undated clipping from the New York *Tribune* in Hastings, Briggs Scrap Book, I, 2-3.

[56] C. A. Briggs, *The Authority of the Holy Scriptures,* pp. 34-35.

[57] Undated clipping from the New York *Tribune* in Hastings, Briggs Scrap Book, I, 2-3.

than matched by the mortification of the visitors. But undaunted, he launched into a fourth barrier to the Bible, the dogma of the authenticity of the Scriptures.[58]

The censure here was aimed at the traditionalists' assumption that the authenticity of the Bible was founded upon the belief that holy men of old had written the various books of Holy Writ. This presupposition was deemed as absolute proof of the veracity of the Sacred Book. "These traditions," said the inaugural speaker, "assign authors to all the books of the Bible, and in the authority of these human writers, it is claimed that the Bible is divine."

The remaining strictures against the traditionalists' position were calculated to fan the audience's furor, already smoldering, to the kindling point. These irritating remarks are important enough for direct quotation:

> But what do we know of the authors apart from the Bible itself? Apart from the sacred writings—Moses and David were not more inspired than Confucius or Sakya Muni. They were leaders of men, but how do we know that they were called of God to speak divine words to us? The only way in which we can prove their authority is from their writings, and yet we are asked to accept the authority of these writings on the authority of these authors.
>
> When such fallacies are thrust in the face of men seeking divine authority in the Bible, is it strange that so many turn away in disgust? It is just here that the Higher Criticism has proved such a terror in our times. Traditionalists are crying out that it is destroying the Bible, because it is exposing their fallacies and follies . . . It may be regarded as the certain result of the science of the Higher Criticism that Moses did not write the Pentateuch or Job; Ezra did not write the Chronicles,

---

[58] This was not the first inaugural of Briggs's that had ruffled orthodox feathers. When made chairman of the Department of Hebrew nearly two decades before, Briggs caused quite a stir with his inaugural address then. See his *Address on the Occasion of the Inauguration as Davenport Professor of Hebrew and the Cognate Languages in the Union Theological Seminary* (New York, 1876), located in the library of Union Theological Seminary.

Ezra or Nehemiah; Jeremiah did not write the Kings or Lamentations; David did not write the Psalter, but only a few of the Psalms; Solomon did not write the Song of Songs or Ecclesiastes, and only a portion of the Proverbs; Isaiah did not write half of the book that bears his name. The great mass of the Old Testament was written by authors whose names or connection with their writings are lost in oblivion.[59]

If Briggs had concluded his address at this point, he could have been certain that the Presbyterian church would take steps to end his career as a minister and teacher in that denomination. But if there were doubts in Briggs's mind, his next words should have eliminated them. He turned his concluding remarks into a call to arms. From this point on, the inaugural address was a manifesto urging all liberals to join in the higher-criticism war against the conservatives. Casting himself in the role of a would-be conqueror, Briggs finished his lecture with a spirited exhortation:

> We have undermined the breastworks of Traditionalism; let us blow them to atoms. We have forged our way through the obstructions; let us remove them now from the face of the earth ... criticism is at work everywhere with knife and fire! Let us cut down everything that is dead and harmful, every kind of dead orthodoxy, every species of effete ecclesiasticism, all mere formal morality, all those dry and brittle fences that constitute denominationalism, and are barriers to church unity.
>
> Let us burn up every form of false doctrine, false religion, and false practice. Let us remove every incumbrance out of the way for a new life; the life of God is moving throughout Christendom, and the spring time of a new age is about to come upon us.[60]

Charles Augustus Briggs had crossed his Rubicon. The traditionalists would not pass up the challenge.

---
[59] C. A. Briggs, *The Authority of the Holy Scriptures*, pp. 32-33.
[60] *Ibid.*, pp. 41, 67.

CHAPTER III

The Conservative Counterattack: The Immediate General Reaction

It is difficult to determine whether Briggs suspected that his controversial address would result in theological warfare. Possibly he did not. But when the challenge came, he responded with enthusiasm.[1] The eventual outcome of the January speech, observed a visiting dignitary from Scotland, was a direct confrontation of the traditionalists and modernists, a battle fought with the weapons of polemical monographs and ecclesiastical trials. All this ultimately produced, said the Scotsman, an "intellectual fermentation of nationally wide proportions."[2] Before 1890 higher criticism had been only a vague threat; now it emerged as a clear and present danger to prevalent Protestant theology.

How the general public would react to the inaugural address had been presaged by audience responses on the night it was delivered. On one hand, Briggs's students had laced his remarks with resounding applause.[3] This enthusiasm was significant for two reasons. First, it was like a straw in the wind showing how a large segment of public opinion would react favorably to Briggs's theories. Second, the applause that came from the younger element of the audience augured that the attempt to reconstruct Protestant theology

---

[1] New York *World,* May 6, 1891. Briggs gave some glimmer that he suspected something big would come of his inaugural when he said he knew it not to be advisable to deliver the speech. Notwithstanding, he was glad "the war had begun."

[2] Unmarked and undated newspaper clipping in Hastings, Briggs Scrap Book, I, 35.

[3] Undated clipping from the New York *Tribune* in Hastings, *ibid.,* I, 2-3.

would have its greatest support from the new and rising generation of ministers.[4]

The reaction of Briggs's students, however, had been more than equaled by the shock of visiting dignitaries. More than any other, the reaction of Dr. William G. T. Shedd, fellow faculty member of Briggs's, anticipated how strongly the old-guard divines would oppose the new theology.[5] Hunched throughout the lecture like a brooding sphinx in his chair on the platform, Shedd barely contained his annoyance.[6] As time would show, his irritation over Briggs's inaugural would register itself in many ways. He became one of the new chairman's severest critics, and in the stormy months ahead he emerged as one of the most effective spokesmen for the orthodox.

The large minority to respond sympathetically to Briggs's statements was typified by a comment in the New York *Tribune*. This leading newspaper expressed its pleasure that higher criticism had at last been given a fair hearing.[7] Similar testimonials of approbation came from areas outside New York City; often they came from remote parts of the world.[8]

What pleasantly surprised liberals and shocked traditionalists was that even some missionaries evinced a sympathy for the new theological departure. One of them, serving in Asia, went so far as to write: "I defy any man to prove the infallibility of the Scriptures."[9]

But the bulk of public reaction was cool towards Briggs's *démarche*. The New York *Observer,* a Presbyterian organ, was provoked because the inaugural speaker had raised reason to a position equal to that of the Bible.[10] Judgments from the hinterland, as might be expected, were more virulent. Rural Pennsylvania, as attested by

---

[4] New York *Sun,* April 12, 1891; New York *Tribune,* November 4, 1891.

[5] Undated newspaper clipping from the New York *Sun* in Hastings, Briggs Scrap Book, I, 72.

[6] Undated clipping from the New York *Tribune* in Hastings, *ibid.,* I, 2-3.

[7] *Ibid.*

[8] Unmarked and undated newspaper clipping in Hastings, *ibid.,* III, 76.

[9] "How It Looks to a Missionary," undated clipping from the New York *Evangelist* in Hastings, *ibid.,* I, 14.

[10] April 30, 1891.

a typical editorial in *Zion's Watchtower,* was hostile. "If we can place no dependence on the inspiration of the language of the Bible," said this journal, "we are entirely without a divine revelation."[11] Greater disaffection was shown by the San Francisco *Occident;* this Presbyterian paper was deeply concerned with the "pugilistic manner in which Briggs had presented" his arguments to the public.[12]

The most vitriolic attack on the January 20 address, however, did not come from either the secular or the religious press. It sprang from one of Briggs's own colleagues, the outraged Dr. William G. T. Shedd.

Compelled by reasons of conscience to refute the inaugural, Shedd determined to "disarm this infidel in Traditionalists' armor." In an article entitled "Conjectural Criticism," this critic attempted to embarrass Briggs by using some of Briggs's methods: if the inaugural speaker could list barriers to the Bible, Shedd could enumerate barriers to the acceptance of higher criticism.[13]

"The first reason why the theory of Higher Criticism is totally untenable," Shedd contended, "was because it is a wholly modern theory." The arch-conservative explained that it was highly improbable that the investigation of biblical scholars for sixteen hundred years should suddenly be demolished by the discoveries of a couple of modern philologists.[14]

The second reason, stated Shedd, was that the German approach to the Bible was a "wholly conjectural science." Until recently, higher criticism had been known only as "conjectural criticism." It deserved this name because it was founded solely upon "theorizing," "the inventiveness of the human intellect," and "ingenuous schemes unsupported by history."[15]

There was still a third reason, continued Briggs's antagonist,

---

[11] Undated clipping in Hastings, Briggs Scrap Book, I, 16-17. This journal was published in Alleghany, Pennsylvania.

[12] April 1, 1891.

[13] "Conjectural Criticism," undated clipping from the New York *Observer* in Hastings, Briggs Scrap Book, I, 4.

[14] *Ibid.*

[15] *Ibid.*

why higher criticism was a baseless science. It divorced biblical inspiration from the traditional writers of the books of the Bible. "The moment therefore that inspiration is severed from known individuals," asserted Shedd, "the moment it is disconnected from the college of prophets and apostles, it becomes an inspiration of the air."[16]

Shedd's attempt to dispute the validity of higher criticism was more an ineffectual plea *ad hominem* than a reasoned refutation. However, his effort was significant because it demonstrated how vulnerable most of the traditionalists' arguments were in the light of modern scholarship. Moreover, Shedd showed that the plainer the inconsistencies of the traditionalists were proven to be, the more reckless their arguments would become. In short, the old-guard theologians in time would resort to polemics rather than reason. This drift was eventually to drive many middle-of-the-roaders into the liberal camp.[17]

The general public reaction against the inaugural, although often caustic, gave Briggs little concern. This was because realistically appraising the situation, he saw that the censures were the work either of critics like Shedd or of journalists throughout the country. Moreover, the initial public response was too sporadic to cause anxiety. Even when put together, the early attacks failed to threaten Briggs's position in the Presbyterian church.

Within three months, however, the situation changed. By April, the inaugural address had caused such a stir that the Presbyterian church itself began to consider what punitive measures should be taken against the professor.

This development arose in part because of the way the issue had been blown up in the press. At first, few newspapers outside New York City carried the story, as it was deemed a local fracas. By April the story was seen to have national implications. The press achieved in three months what Briggs probably could not have accomplished in three years of public lectures.[18]

---

[16] *Ibid.*

[17] "Is Professor Briggs a Heretic?" New York *Sun,* April 12, 1891; New York *Observer,* May 28, 1891; New York *Evangelist,* October 29, 1891.

[18] Charles Butler, chairman of Union's directorate, had persuaded the seminary to arrange for Briggs's inaugural address at a very auspicious time.

The Charles A. Briggs Heresy Trial

Briggs and higher criticism were about to be enshrined on the pages of American intellectual history. Action soon to be taken by the General Assembly of the Presbyterian Church made this a certainty.

Nothing of great importance was happening in January, 1891; in fact, the whole year was largely uneventful. Newspapers were glad of the Briggs case because it gave them something to write about. Because of the news vacuum, the secular newspapers inadvertently became important allies of Briggs in the spreading of German ideas. If the Briggs case had begun one year earlier, it probably would have been overshadowed in the newspapers by the Sherman Anti-Trust and Silver Purchase acts. If the higher criticism inaugural had been delayed one year, Briggs would have had to compete with the boisterous presidential campaign of 1892. The year 1891 was thus an excellent year in which to launch the higher criticism movement in America. Newspapers starved for stories spotlighted higher criticism in 1891 just about as effectively as the radio publicized Darwinism at the time of the Scopes trail a generation later. See Richard B. Morris (editor), *Encyclopedia of American History* (New York, 1961), pp. 261-263, 284.

CHAPTER IV

The Conservative Counterattack: The Detroit General Assembly

The reaction against Briggs that caught the eye of the press and hence effectively publicized higher criticism was the official action of the Presbyterian church. In contrast to isolated strictures described in the previous chapter, this movement caused Briggs serious concern.

The official castigation was significant for two reasons. First, as an official reproof, it caused considerable consternation to both Briggs and his supporters. The second reason logically flows from the first: because the official action of the Presbyterian church constituted an effective censure, Briggs's sympathizers were forced to intensify their efforts in his behalf.[1] The net result was a strong and articulate counterreaction in favor of the inaugural and higher criticism. The activities of this pro-Briggs faction demonstrate that higher criticism had penetrated in depth into certain segments of American thought before the beginning of the present century.

The official assault on Briggs by the Presbyterian church consisted of two thrusts, each powerful enough in itself to give the Union professor and his friends pause. One prong, aimed at Briggs as a teacher and at Union Seminary for harboring a heretic, came from the General Assembly. The second push, directed at Briggs as a minister, was initiated by the presbytery of New York City.[2]

---

[1] "Is Professor Briggs a Heretic?" New York *Sun*, April 12, 1891; "In His Own Defense," New York *World*, May 6, 1891, in Hastings, Briggs Scrap Book, I, 8.

[2] The first attack (the Detroit General Assembly) was launched in May with the veto of Briggs's professorship and was continued with varying de-

As time went on these two official campaigns became so intertwined that by 1892 the charges of both attacks were difficult to separate. Nevertheless, for purposes of clarity the two actions that sprang from different groups must be explored in separate order.

Curiously enough, the first pressure put on Briggs by the Presbyterian church did not originate in New York City and its environs. The first official attack, engineered by the General Assembly, came as a result of prodding by midwestern church elements.[3]

The focal point of the midwestern push to "get Briggs" was Cincinnati. Just as the presbytery of New York City was to become the champion of liberalism in the months and years to come, so Cincinnati was to emerge as the hub of anti-higher criticism activity. Accordingly, Cincinnati was possibly the first presbytery to petition the General Assembly to take prompt action against Briggs.[4] In April a petition from Cincinnati urged the Assembly to punish the "eastern heretic" in the name of doctrinal purity.[5] Other midwestern presbyteries promptly followed suit and registered vigorous disapprovals with the Assembly.[6] Especially scathing in their denunciations were presbyteries located in Tennessee and Missouri.[7]

This flow of petitions to the General Assembly demonstrated that these midwesterners were determined that Briggs should be punished.[8] By the time the Assembly convened in the middle of May, over seventy presbyteries (mostly midwestern) had reported

---

grees of intensity through October, by which time the Detroit assault was frustrated. The second attack (New York City presbytery trial) began in April, picked up momentum in May with the decision to try Briggs, and reached its peak on November 4 with the famous first trial of Briggs. Both assaults were checkmated by Christmas of 1891.

[3] "Is Professor Briggs a Heretic?"

[4] Undated Clipping from the Pittsburgh *Presbyterian Banner* in Hastings, Briggs Scrap Book, III, 2.

[5] "Want Dr. Briggs Investigated," unmarked newspaper clipping dated April 22, 1891, in Hastings, *Ibid.*, II, 57-59.

[6] New York *Tribune,* October 5, 1891.

[7] New York *Sun,* April 12, 1891.

[8] "Still Another Overture," unmarked newspaper clipping dated May 9, 1891, in Hastings, Briggs Scrap Book, III, 16.

The Charles A. Briggs Heresy Trial

their dissatisfaction with Briggs's teachings.[9] What produced alarm back east was that this movement to remove Briggs comprehended a wide sphere of cooperation. The hinterland's cooperating circle extended from Iowa to parts of Pennsylvania.[10]

Most presbyteries had not been specific in recommending what action should be taken. There was a vague consensus that the General Assembly should institute measures to remove the unorthodox churchman from his professorship.[11]

Some obdurate presbyteries struck upon a legal way through which Briggs could be removed. The Compact of 1870, which had adjoined Union to other Presbyterian seminaries, clearly stipulated that the General Assembly had the power to pass on the elections of professors in schools under its jurisdiction.[12] The midwesterners also saw a theological way to eliminate Briggs: the Westminster Confession would demonstrate his heterodoxy. A simple comparison of the inaugural with that standard would clearly demonstrate heresy.[13]

Dr. Philip Schaff, Professor of Church History at Union and close friend of Briggs,[14] posited some interesting motives for the

---

[9] "Comments on the General Assembly's Action and Temper," unmarked and undated newspaper clipping in Hastings, *ibid.*, I, 37-39.

[10] "Turn Him Out," undated clipping from the New York *Mail and Express* in Hastings, *ibid.*, III, 15; "Still Another Overture"; "Dr. Briggs Arraigned," undated clipping from the New York *Commercial* in Hastings, *ibid.*, I, 73.

[11] "Fearless of Criticism," undated clipping from the New York *Tribune* in Hastings, *ibid.*, I, 18.

[12] *Ibid.* The midwestern presbyteries had apparently for the moment forgotten that the General Assembly did not have clear constitutional power to pass on "transfers of professors within Union." The General Assembly did have the power to sanction or disapprove of elections of new professors. This subtle distinction was ultimately to be the undoing of the Detroit attack against Briggs.

[13] "Fearless of Criticism."

[14] A liberal in every area of theology, Schaff was a natural ally of Briggs. His liberal bent in issues other than higher criticism was shown in 1870. In that year Schaff enthusiastically accepted an invitation to represent all American Protestants in a conference at Bonn, Germany. The purpose of this conference was to promote Christian unity among Catholics, Greek

midwestern ferment. This German-trained historian said that one reason was "the defiant and exasperating tone" in which Briggs had delivered the address.[15] "It sounded," remarked Schaff, "like a manifesto of war."[16] He added, however, that this in itself did not really explain the violent spirit with which the Midwest reacted to the inaugural address. The real reason stemmed from the Midwest's unquestioning faith in the Bible.[17] The hinterland Protestants feared rationalism as if it were a plague. These Christians were horrified at the prospect that Briggs might open the way "for teaching of downright rationalism in a leading institution of the Presbyterian Church."[18] This "theologicophobia," added to "Germanophobia," impelled "more than seventy presbyteries to petition the General Assembly for stern action against Briggs."[19]

Briggs's eastern sympathizers were quick to discern the storm clouds gathering in the West. Though most midwestern presbyteries couched their petitions in ambiguous words, Briggs's partisans recognized that the object was "to call into question Briggs's appointment to the new chair."[20] By April a cadre of easterners realized that this meant his dismissal from Union's faculty.[21] Just before the Detroit General Assembly was convoked a month later, these protests mounted to the point where the New York *Sun* remarked "there is good reason to believe Briggs is going to be a nineteenth

---

Orthodox Catholics, and Protestants. As with higher criticism, Schaff showed himself therein to be years ahead of his contemporaries in promoting what amounted to ecumenicism. Informed, cautious, given to the measured statement, he was qualified to describe the American Protestant "mind," whether east or west, on the matter of higher criticism.

[15] Philip Schaff, "Other Heresy Trials and the Briggs Case," undated article in Hastings, Briggs Scrap Book, III, 5-6.

[16] *Loc. cit.*

[17] A good study of the Protestant mind in the Midwest and South at the end of the nineteenth century is Kenneth K. Bailey, "Southern White Protestantism at the Turn of the Century," *American Historical Review*, LXVIII (April, 1963), 618-635.

[18] Schaff, "Other Heresy Trials and the Briggs Case."

[19] *Ibid.*

[20] "Fearless of Criticism."

[21] New York *Sun*, April 12, 1891.

century version of Servetus at the hands of the General Assembly at Detroit next week."[22]

Increasingly aware of the intense midwestern movement to expel the Union scholar, the pro-higher criticism groups in the East (especially in New York City) realized that a countermove in behalf of their leader was necessary; otherwise, the Midwest would achieve its objective easily, and the plans to liberalize American theology, if not discredited, would suffer a serious setback.[23]

The pro-Briggs coalition drawn from New York City and environs began to assume impressive proportions. This movement clearly reveals how far higher criticism had penetrated into certain circles of American religious thought in an era generally marked by conservatism.

The first to take the lead in Briggs's behalf was the directorate of Union Theological Seminary. In an attempt to close ranks behind its professor before the convening of the Assembly in May, the board of directors published eight categorical questions asked of Briggs concerning his orthodoxy and the replies he had given.[24] That the questions were so framed as not to force the professor to comment directly on his basic convictions was not realized till later. The immediate impression, however, was that the heretical teacher was not heretical after all. But more important, the board's solicitous attitude demonstrated that Union would stand firmly behind the accused. Though mystifying to midwesterners at first, such intransigence later became understandable when it was disclosed that nearly all faculty members at Union were solidly committed to the larger implications of biblical criticism.[25]

Meanwhile, another concerted effort came to the support of Briggs. Added to the action of the directors of Union, it gave the

---

[22] "Defenders of Professor Briggs," undated clipping from the New York *Sun* in Hastings, Briggs Scrap Book, I, 14.

[23] "Dr. Briggs's Colleagues," unmarked newspaper clipping dated May 27, 1891, in Hastings, *ibid.*, I, 17.

[24] "The Union Seminary and Dr. Briggs," unmarked and undated newspaper clippings in Hastings, *ibid.*, I, 6.

[25] "The Conference," undated clipping from the Cincinnati *Herald and Presbyter* in Hastings, *ibid.*, I, 33.

pro-Briggs counterthrust an impressive dimension. Union's alumni were invited to join forces with their alma mater to withstand the midwestern assault in the General Assembly.

Of the 217 alumni to respond,[26] 176 were in favor of Briggs, and urged that a formal request be made to the General Assembly not to remove Briggs from his post.[27] But even more revealing than these statistics are explanatory letters which were attached to some of the responses. The comment by Rev. Herbert G. Lord of Buffalo, New York, is typical: "I am heart and head with Dr. Briggs, and so will everybody else in due time."

What pleasantly surprised Union's board of directors, however, was that a number of sympathetic letters came from the Midwest. This disclosed that despite the way in which this region regarded the Bible, higher criticism had indeed crossed the Alleghenies.

To be sure, letters coming from Cincinnati—the "self-appointed center of mid-western orthodoxy"—were few and far between. But all around Cincinnati there were conclaves of liberal dissent. To the northeast, left-wing theological sentiment was manifested in a letter which came from Dr. Edward P. Cleaveland, professor at Adelbert College in Cleveland: "The effort to remove Dr. Briggs would be disastrous to the cause of Truth."[28] Similar thoughts came in a letter from a Brooklyn, Iowa, pastor who ardently declared his sympathy for Briggs and the higher criticism movement.[29] From Kearney, Nebraska, came another declaration for Briggs which asserted that he was definitely not to be considered "a dangerous teacher simply because of the contents of his Inaugural."[30] And to the south of Cincinnati, Rev. James E. Rogers of Maryville, Tennessee, protested: "I do not fear the conclusions of Dr. Briggs's investigations."[31]

The most unexpected response from the Midwest—unexpected

---

[26] "How It Looks to the Alumni," unmarked and undated newspaper clipping in Hastings, *ibid.*, I, 6.

[27] *Ibid.*

[28] *Ibid.*

[29] *Ibid.*

[30] *Ibid.*

[31] *Ibid.*

The Charles A. Briggs Heresy Trial

because it came from the center of hostility to higher criticism—stemmed from Dr. Arthur C. McGiffert of Lane Seminary in Cincinnati.[32] Although McGiffert's trained eye detected strong traces of German theology in the inaugural, he said, "I regard Dr. Briggs as one of the most helpful and inspiring teachers in our Church."[33]

An impressive majority of the *Presbyterian* alumni contacted were in some measure in accord with Briggs's espousal of higher criticism. But enthusiastically in agreement were all *Congregational* alumni.[34] Significantly, most of these Congregational graduates came from the East.[35] Typical was Rev. William E. Griffis of Boston, who hailed Briggs's brave stand because of "the powerful influence for good he is exerting upon the educated Christian mind of the country."[36] In the same spirit Rev. John L. Scudder of Jersey City, New Jersey, replied that Briggs's theological doctrines impressed him as "progressive and thoroughly constructive."[37] The *Dutch-Reformed* alumni fully concurred with these favorable sentiments of their Congregational brethren.[38]

With barely a week to go before the convening of the Detroit General Assembly, the pro-Briggs phalanx was formed in full and ready to fight. On the surface it looked like a motley group, constituted as it was of men scattered throughout the country and emanating from various denominations. But the group coalesced with great intensity as opposition delegates began to converge at

---

[32] Lane Seminary, which was virtually an island of liberalism surrounded by the sea of the reactionary Cincinnati presbytery, had a comparably long history of being at the forefront of liberal movements. Lane, for instance, had been a center of pre-Civil War abolitionism. See "Lane Seminary," unmarked and undated newspaper clipping in Hastings, Briggs Scrap Book, IV, 5; "A Friendly Caution," Hastings, *ibid.*, IV, 4; New York *Sun*, April 3, 1892.

[33] "How It Looks to the Alumni."

[34] *Ibid.* Thirty-seven Congregational ministers were contacted. Their liberalism is not too difficult to explain since, unlike Presbyterians, they were not answerable to a central body for their theological opinions.

[35] *Ibid.*
[36] *Ibid.*
[37] *Ibid.*
[38] *Ibid.*

Detroit. Moreover, the pro-Briggs group enjoyed the support of articulate intellectuals who possessed reformers' zeal to liberalize Protestant theology.

Nonetheless, Union Seminary, still fearful of midwestern strength in the General Assembly, decided to utilize the few intervening days to strengthen its position even more. In an attempt to reiterate that Briggs's January 20 address had not deviated fundamentally from the Westminster Confession, the seminary published an amplified version of the accused professor's beliefs on the Bible.[39] Still another last-minute measure came when the directorate of Union told the press that the seminary planned to present "a strong presentation" in Dr. Briggs's behalf in their annual report to the Assembly.[40]

Meanwhile, the traditionalists had not been moved by the arguments of the pro-Briggs coalition nor diverted by Union's stratagem. However Union tries to gloss over the inaugural, asserted one of their number, they cannot excuse Briggs's higher critical principles nor his loose views on Scripture in general.[41]

There were good reasons why the conservatives were not beguiled. If Briggs possessed uncanny sagacity in theology, he was a novice in church politics. At the moment when Union's tactics were beginning to be efficacious, Briggs injudiciously decided to make a radical comment to the press on the Book of Daniel. Blind to the maxims of statecraft, he made indiscreet assertions to the effect that the prophet Daniel had never written the book accredited to his name; rather, it was written by some unknown redactor who lived much later than the supposed author.[42]

With unflagging zeal, Briggs committed another ill-timed blunder. In a long statement to a reporter designed to clarify his theological position, he indulged himself *à l'improviste*. Extemporization was a strong weapon in the hands of a man like Briggs's friend, the cool-headed Dr. Philip Schaff, but in the hands of the

---

[39] "Defenders of Professor Briggs."
[40] "His Colleagues Defend Dr. Briggs," undated clipping from the New York *Herald* in Hastings, Briggs Scrap Book, I, 15.
[41] "Dr. Briggs's Colleagues."
[42] "Art Thou That Daniel?" New York *Observer,* April 2, 1891.

The Charles A. Briggs Heresy Trial

accused professor it became an instrument of self-destruction. Overcome by emotion, Briggs blurted out, "The Bible is not inerrant."[43] He went on to compound this blunder by extolling the "German-trained Higher Critics on the Continent" for their imaginative and progressive discoveries in the field of biblical scholarship.[44]

Needless to say, these badly timed statements pulled the rug from under Union Seminary's valiant attempt to set up a defense against the Midwest's determined plan to persuade the General Assembly to remove Briggs from his chair.

Meanwhile, Briggs's arch-critic in New York City, Dr. Shedd, once more took up the cudgels. In a widely read rejoinder to Briggs's recent press statement, Shedd further harmed Union's scheme to protect its professor at Detroit. Whereas Shedd's previous rebuttals had been ineffectual because they were marked more by emotion than by fact, his latest effusion was a convincing demonstration of the theological inconsistencies existing between Briggs's public statements and the Westminster Confession.[45] Shedd's exposé was cleverly timed to persuade the fence sitters in the forthcoming General Assembly to join forces with the western delegates.

If Shedd's sense of timing was precise, his assumption that Briggs had not a "corporal's guard behind him" was wrong.[46] The anonymous author of an article entitled "The Theological Contest" was much closer to the truth when he declared, "Briggs is really at the head of a great party which has been forming for some time now from all branches of Protestantism."[47]

Nor was Shedd's timing altogether correct. To be sure, it did have immediate effects; but as the New York *Times* put it, "time is ultimately on the side of Briggs," whether or not Shedd and his cohorts wished to recognize it. Briggs represented, argued the *Times,* an intellectual movement which was sweeping the world, not

---

[43] New York *World,* May 6, 1891
[44] *Ibid.*
[45] "Dr. Briggs Draws Fire," New York *World,* May 8, 1891.
[46] *Ibid.*
[47] "The Theological Contest," unmarked and undated article in Hastings, Briggs Scrap Book, I, 40.

only the United States of America.[48] If Shedd anticipated that the Detroit General Assembly would root out higher criticism once and for all by banishing its directing genius in America, he was nursing an illusion. German theology had cut so deeply into American intellectual circles that one journal was able to foretell with amazing accuracy what the role of the Detroit General Assembly would be. "At the Detroit General Assembly," predicted this paper, "only the skirmish lines between the opponents and proponents of the Higher Criticism will be engaged. The general action which will follow the General Assembly will be of long continuance."[49]

These "skirmish lines" had indeed been forming well in advance of the Detroit General Assembly. Evidence of a solid midwestern front against Briggs was ascertained by a curious reporter representing the New York *Mail and Express*. Shortly after adjournment of the Detroit Assembly, this newsman arranged to make pointed inquiries of some of the western delegates. Particularly illuminating was information garnered from a Missouri delegate who had traveled to Detroit on a train loaded with over a hundred fellow-western delegates.

The Missouri commissioner related he had asked some one hundred and fifty deputies, coming from such cities as Cincinnati, Chicago, St. Louis, Milwaukee, and Cleveland, how they stood on Briggs. Not one of them said they sympathized with the heretic.[50] The significance of the Missourian's reply, if true, is not difficult to assess. It demonstrates, first of all, the solidarity of midwestern hostility against higher criticism. Second, it suggests that the inland delegates had been chosen primarily, if not solely, because they could be counted on to oppose Briggs in the General Assembly.[51] The suspicion that the Detroit convocation had been packed was documented later when a Rev. James S. Ramsey, himself an anti-Briggs man at Detroit, confessed that most of the anti-Briggs

---

[48] "What Dr. Briggs's Case Implies," New York *Times,* May 17, 1891.
[49] "The Theological Contest."
[50] "Briggsdoxy: The Union Seminary Should Free Itself from It," unmarked and undated newspaper clipping in Hastings Briggs Scrap Book, I, 44-45.
[51] "Fearless of Criticism."

people had been elected to that body with the understanding that they would steadfastly oppose the New York teacher.[52]

The midwestern delegates were not the only ones to come to Detroit with closed minds. There were also the eastern conferees. But unlike the hinterland delegates whose minds had been made up for them by their presbyteries, the seaboard commissioners came to Michigan with determined convictions of their own making.[53] That this was the case was substantiated by the investigations of a New York *Herald* reporter.

In a number of interviews, this newsman discovered that most of the eastern representatives sympathized with a Mr. Nelson of the Memorial Presbyterian Church of Brooklyn. Without hesitation Nelson declared, "I do not believe Briggs's views in the Inaugural are really against the Westminster Confession."[54]

Evincing a similar sentiment, another man from the seaboard replied, "It was my privilege to be one of a large company of clergymen representing different branches of the Church, with whom Professor Briggs was invited to dine a few weeks ago. The impression he made was as delightful as it was profound. We paid him the willing tribute of our confidence, and our admiration for his splendid scholarship."[55]

This interviewer from the *Herald* not only discovered that the bulk of eastern delegates were pro-Briggs; he also corroborated the findings of his colleague from the *Mail and Express* that the midwesterners regarded their trip to Detroit as a safari to bring home the head of the king of American higher critics. There was no question in the mind of Rev. S. M. Johnson, a pastor from Denver,

---

[52] "Not the Assembly's Business," unmarked and undated newspaper clipping in Hastings, Briggs Scrap Book, I, 15-16.

[53] Proof that Briggs had stirred a great interest in higher criticism by May was shown by the fact that reporters from leading New York papers were assigned to find out what the issue was all about. Just as the New York *Mail and Express* reporter discovered that midwestern delegates were unanimously anti-higher criticism, so the New York *Herald* correspondent found the eastern commissioners to be pro-higher criticism.

[54] "Clergy on the Case," unmarked and undated newspaper clipping in Hastings, Briggs Scrap Book, I, 52-53.

[55] *Ibid.*

Colorado, that Briggs should be punished because he was clearly "against the Westminster Confession."[56] Delegate A. W. Ringland of Duluth, Minnesota, was equally eager to put an end to the Briggs menace.[57]

Perhaps it was best that Briggs decided against going to Detroit in order to defend himself in person.[58] It was unlikely that he could have moved the intransigent westerners. It is safe to say, however, that he probably would have enjoyed the city of Detroit itself. Especially delightful and charming was the area in which the General Assembly convened. Serene and stately Woodward Avenue, lined with freshly mown lawns and shaded by giant elm trees and graced with elegant Victorian homes, was an impressive site for the proceedings about to begin.[59]

The rustling leaves and drowsy summer sun, however, had not lulled everybody into an illusion that all was tranquil within the walls of the Woodward Avenue Presbyterian Church, the place of the Detroit convocation. A local wit, blessed with the gift of cynicism, observed that it was ironic that "this city which had been settled around the time of the religious ferment of the Thirty Years' War was about to become two hundred and eighty years later the scene of another religious fracas."[60] Only this time it was Protestant against Protestant, not Catholic against Protestant!

The quipster's comparison was slightly exaggerated, but no one could deny that the city was astir. In previous years delegates had been notoriously negligent in their assembly duties; bored to death, they had more often than not slept through the proceedings. In the 1891 General Assembly, however, not one conferee was caught dozing. From the very first day of the meetings to the last, the atmosphere seemed charged with electricity generated by a battery of words.[61]

---

[56] *Ibid.*

[57] *Ibid.*

[58] Undated clipping from the New York *Evangelist* in Hastings, Briggs Scrap Book, I, 67.

[59] "The Storm Center at Detroit," New York *Evangelist,* June 4, 1891.

[60] "The Briggs Controversy," unmarked and undated newspaper clipping in Hastings, Briggs Scrap Book, I, 62-63.

[61] "The Storm Center at Detroit."

The Charles A. Briggs Heresy Trial

How things were to go for Briggs was indicated when, on the first day, Dr. William Henry Green, Professor of Theology at Princeton Seminary, was elected moderator.[62] To outsiders this selection meant nothing; however, to members of the Assembly who understood church politics, Green's election was proof that the midwesterners were out to build an efficient machine by which to crush Briggs's defenders. Princeton Seminary, inflexibly dedicated to the orthodox path blazed by its short-time president, Jonathan Edwards, was a citadel of correct Presbyterian doctrine. As an eastern paper remarked, "Princeton is the admitted home of Presbyterian orthodoxy, where successive generations of massive intellects have met and defeated error and have earnestly contended for the Faith Once Delivered to the Saints."[63]

Thus Green's selection was properly regarded as a clear-cut midwestern victory. It was a fair indication of what was to happen during the remainder of the gathering. This was so because, inasmuch as Union Seminary had long been recognized as the rallying point for liberal Presbyterians, the New York institution was the natural enemy of Princeton Seminary.[64] Princeton's Dr. Green was strongly opposed to Briggs for two reasons. First, Briggs had deviated from the orthodox standard of the Church; second, he belonged to a school long disliked by Princeton. The Midwest had played its trump card and won: it had manipulated Princeton into being a front to help achieve its purposes. The Princeton-western axis had been forged impressively.

Nothing else of consequence happened until May 28, the first of three days which the General Assembly allotted to consider the Briggs case.[65] On that day another action occurred which more than ever made Briggs's chances look bleak. Moderator Green announced the names of fifteen men whom he had picked for the committee to deliberate on the Briggs matter—that is, the Committee on Theological Seminaries. The makeup of this Committee

---

[62] *Ibid.*
[63] New York *Herald,* October 18, 1891.
[64] "Commentary on the Briggs Case," San Francisco *Occident,* November 25, 1891, in Hastings, Briggs Scrap Book, II, inside front cover.
[65] "The Storm Center at Detroit.

revealed much. It underscored how the Midwest and Princeton, poles apart in gentility, had momentarily forgotten their differences to make common cause against the chief apostle of higher criticism.[66] When Moderator Green read the names of the fifteen men, his audience at once realized that every selectee was opposed to Briggs's doctrines.[67] In other words, Green had packed the committee to guarantee a proper decision.[68]

Green rubbed salt into the wounds of the liberals when he chose Dr. Francis Landey Patton as chairman of the committee. Patton was notorious for being a heresy hunter,[69] and in addition was president of Princeton College![70] A Princeton moderator had selected the president of Princeton to make certain an orthodox victory.

Reactions to this choice were strong and immediate. The New York *Evening Post* asserted that the committee was little more than a screen for the Midwest to achieve its aim in suppressing higher criticism.[71] Another New York newspaper echoed these sentiments when it later observed: "The Briggs trial was doubly unfair; first, because Briggs himself was not there to defend himself . . . secondly, because Briggs did not have so much as one defender on the Committee."[72] Most of the secular press concurred that "the decent thing in this situation would have been either to have postponed the investigation or have one of the ablest easterners defend Briggs." But the Princeton-western alliance would not bend ear to these suggestions. It was all too clear that they were out to get Briggs "so that he could not come to life again to trouble them hereafter."[73]

The mounting criticism, which came from both East and Mid-

---

[66] "The Briggs Case," New York *Evening Post*, November 5, 1891.

[67] "The Storm Center at Detroit."

[68] *Ibid.*

[69] New York *Recorder*, November 3, 1891.

[70] "Directors Stand Firm," unmarked and undated newspaper clipping in Hastings, Briggs Scrap Book, I, 29.

[71] "The Briggs Case."

[72] New York *Evangelist*, June 25, 1891.

[73] *Ibid.*

west,[74] would have given a lesser man pause, but not Chairman Patton. The Princeton president, sometimes called an American Torquemada, engineered a swift decision against the Union professor.[75] But not everything went Patton's way. Before the vote was rammed through, Patton was forced to bow to at least a semblance of constitutionalism. The result was that in a plenary session, the General Assembly played witness to one of the "greatest theological debates" in American history,[76] a debate that clearly demonstrated that the early higher criticism movement in America possessed formidable proportions.

The most stirring address in behalf of Briggs was delivered by Dr. Henry Preserved Smith, Professor of Hebrew at Lane Seminary. This learned Hebraist electrified the delegates when he pointed out that even the "purest of purest," the late Dr. Charles Hodge of Princeton Seminary,[77] whose orthodoxy remained unquestioned, had in unguarded moments shown evidence of higher criticism's effect upon his thinking. Smith used Hodge as a means to indict the commissioners before him of hypocrisy when he said, "You condemn Dr. Briggs for holding to Higher Criticism . . . but did you know that Dr. Hodge without reservation classed Schleiermacher as a Christian? You may ask who Schleiermacher was. He was a German rationalist . . . who held to a doctrine of inspiration which would be considered by this Assembly as decidedly loose. Now if Dr. Hodge could put this rationalist in Heaven, shall we condemn Dr. Briggs . . . for his views on Higher Criticism?"[78]

If Smith's indictment of Hodge shook the anti-higher criticism delegates, his arraignment of Dr. Benjamin Warfield numbed them.

---

[74] "The Storm Center at Detroit"; also see undated clipping from the *Outlook* in Hastings, Briggs Scrap Book, I, 71-72.

[75] Undated clipping from the *Outlook* in Hastings, ibid., I, 71-72.

[76] "Professor Briggs is Sustained by Union," New York *Sun,* June 6, 1891.

[77] More than any other scholar, Dr. Charles Hodge gave classic expression to Princeton theology. His masterly and prolific writings on various phases of theology "constituted a late-autumn harvest of American Calvinism." See Lefferts A. Loetscher, *The Broadening Church* (Philadelphia, 1954), pp. 23-24.

[78] Clippings of minutes and comments concerning the proceedings of the Detroit General Assembly (1891) in Hastings, Briggs Scrap Book, I, 22-23.

"You condemn Briggs for arguing against the Doctrine of the Inerrance of the Scriptures. Yet you not only fully endorse Hodge as the belated guardian of orthodoxy, but also the present Princeton guardian of orthodoxy as beyond reproach . . . Professor Benjamin Warfield. But did you know that, because of the findings of Higher Criticism, he had adjudged the last twelve verses of the Gospel of Mark as not part of Scripture, that they are corruptions of the text?"[79] Smith also pointed out that Warfield likewise held the famous text in the Gospel of John on the adulterous woman to be spurious. Folding his manuscript, he concluded, "You will condemn Dr. Briggs for not believing in the inerrancy of the original Scriptures, yet fully believe in Dr. Warfield who affirms corruptions in the transmission in the text of the New Testament in such important particulars as I have stated. Ought you not in consistency pronounce also against the views of Dr. Warfield?" There was some astonishment when Smith received rousing applause.[80]

Smith's discourse came like a bolt of lightning in the dark, for it illuminated the fact that many orthodox theologians were guilty of harboring higher criticism sentiments. Moreover, Smith revealed something else: the applause which punctuated his speech gave rise to the suspicion that more delegates than had been surmised nurtured a secret sympathy for modern German theology.

This suspicion mounted when a leading conservative Presbyterian journal in the East admitted that Briggs had won over a large secret following, constituted not only of "avowed antagonists of the evangelical religion, but also many ministers and laymen who were truly evangelical."[81] Though no effort was made to explain the term "evangelical," informed Protestants held it to be a synonym for orthodoxy.[82]

Sensing that the term evangelical needed precise definition, Dr. Willis J. Beecher of Auburn Theological Seminary[83] later gave

---

[79] *Ibid.*

[80] *Ibid.*

[81] "Is It a Retraction?" New York *Observer*, May 28, 1891.

[82] Herrick Johnson, "Confounding Things that Differ," unmarked and undated newspaper clipping in Hastings, Briggs Scrap Book, I, 25-26.

[83] Auburn Seminary in Auburn, New York, was another of the Presby-

an enlightening exposition. He explained that the "whole evangelical spectrum" had been influenced to one degree or another by higher criticism. Logic demanded, he remarked sardonically, that the verdict against Briggs be placed against "every exegetical scholar in the Presbyterian Church."[84] Such an all-encompassing verdict was in order, Beecher added, because virtually all leading American theologians acceded to the validity of Wellhausen's hypotheses.[85] The only difference between Briggs and the rest of the avant-garde theologians was that Briggs stood to the left of the spectrum of evangelicalism. Many of the very accusers of Briggs, despite public utterances to the contrary, were influenced by the Berlin theology. Beecher grew specific when he said that a list of such possible heretics would include even the distinguished moderator of the Detroit General Assembly.

Such a bold accusation needed factual support. Documentation was not wanting. It had already been shown that the Princeton theologian had written articles in which he made generous concessions to German learning. Most bewildering of all was one in which he admitted that verbal inspiration was a historical impossibility.[86] Beecher concluded, "From my point of view, the difference between the position of many conservative theologians and Professor Briggs on Higher Criticism may be resolved into a difference of degree. It is simply that Briggs's concessions of error are more numerous than theirs."[87]

It seemed that Beecher, like Briggs, was inviting martyrdom. But Beecher knew that the facts were on his side.[88] His indictment was soon vindicated. Many scholars agreed that a demand for a verdict against Briggs required similar verdicts against all exegeti-

---

terian church's theological schools. See Lefferts A. Loetscher, *The Broadening Church* (Philadelphia, 1954), pp. 74-82, for an excellent discussion of the Presbyterian church's seminaries and how they developed.

[84] Willis J. Beecher, "The Situation," unmarked and undated article in Hastings, Briggs Scrap Book, I, 27-28.

[85] *Ibid.*

[86] "Those Specks of Sandstone in the Marble of the Parthenon," New York *Evangelist*, July 2, 1891.

[87] "The Situation."

[88] *Ibid.*

cal scholars. Dr. Herrick Johnson, an esteemed Chicago theologian, was typical; he said he was in full accord with Beecher and added that he knew of a "host of Presbyterian ministers . . . who belong to a group that should be known as 'Evangelical Higher Critics.' "[89]

Professor Henry Preserved Smith's plea in behalf of Briggs had thus sparked a dialogue which dramatically demonstrated that higher criticism had cut even into the circle of the Princeton untouchables.

Although Smith's address moved many moderates in the Detroit General Assembly, it did not so much as stir a ripple among the die-hard traditionalists. This was probably because Smith himself had long been suspected of higher criticism leanings. But if Smith left the reactionaries cold, Dr. Bartlett, an arch-conservative from Washington, D.C., left them at least uncomfortable.

It was Bartlett's job to refute Smith and denounce Briggs. But the trouble was that the more he talked, the more he disconcerted his fellow conservatives with unwitting concessions to German discoveries. In an attempt to telescope the history of higher criticism into a ten-minute summary, the Washington minister noted that some seven or eight hundred theories as to the authorship of the Pentateuch were in vogue. Was it not much better, he asked, to believe that Moses had written the first five books of the Old Testament? "What makes the difference between a level-headed Traditionalist and a typsy Higher Critic," he remarked histrionically, "is that a Traditionalist will remember that he is not ordained to discover whether Moses wrote the Pentateuch . . . because the problem of the authorship of the Pentateuch may be a question of such delicacy and difficulty that it could not be absolutely and finally settled."[90] Then, apparently realizing his unwitting concession to higher criticism, Bartlett stopped, fumbled nervously with his notes, and refused to discuss the matter further. Somewhat embarrassed, he tried to save face by stating that Christian ministers

---

[89] "Confounding Things that Differ."

[90] Clipping of minutes and comments concerning the proceedings of the Detroit General Assembly (1891) in Hastings, Briggs Scrap Book, I, 22-23.

The Charles A. Briggs Heresy Trial 61

were not ordained to discover whether Moses wrote the Pentateuch but rather to preach the gospel.[91]

Despite these demonstrations that higher criticism had influenced the entire spectrum of Presbyterianism, Patton prodded his committee into drawing up the indictment against Briggs. The Princeton president would let nothing get in the way of Briggs's dismissal in spite of the preponderant sentiment in the Assembly favoring leniency.

Still other factors should have prompted restraint in Patton. A few days before the Assembly convened, Union had been promised by leaders in that body that an indictment would not be brought against Briggs if the Seminary's board secured from him a statement on his loyalty to the Westminster Confession.[92] This, Union had done.[93] In addition, Patton should have recalled the nature of the Compact of 1870. This compact, which linked Union to the Presbyterian denomination, was very ambiguous as to the kind of control the General Assembly was to enjoy over the New York school. There was no question that the larger body possessed the right to pass on elections of new professors.[94] But there was much debate whether the same was applicable to transfers of professors from one department to another.[95] Briggs had been transferred to his new post, not elected.

That Union Seminary had the better of the legal argument on the transfer was admitted by almost everyone.[96] Even Patton grasped this point. Retreating in the face of hard facts, he stalled

---

[91] *Ibid.*

[92] "Union Stands by Briggs," unmarked and undated newspaper clipping in Hastings, Briggs Scrap Book, I, 32.

[93] Llewellyn J. Evans, "No Reasons," unmarked and undated newspaper clipping in Hastings, *ibid.,* I, 21.

[94] *Ibid.* Both parties of the contract made concessions and had something to gain. Union was to be guaranteed Presbyterian patronage in students and money; the General Assembly was to exercise general control over the New York school.

[95] Clipping of minutes and comments concerning the proceedings of the Detroit General Assembly (1891) in Hastings, Briggs Scrap Book, I, 22-23.

[96] Schaff, "Other Heresy Trials and the Briggs Case."

the indictment process against Briggs long enough for an *ad hoc* Committee of Conference to investigate the matter. This special committee's findings were to be reported to the Committee on Theological Seminaries as soon as possible.[97] But in the end Patton's fundamentalist obscurantism got the best of him. Annoyed that constitutionalism was protecting a heretic, the Princeton professor refused to wait for the special report and pushed ahead for a quick decision against Briggs.[98] Chairman Patton rationalized this precipitate action by saying that "according to established precedents, unless the Assembly disapproved the election at this time, it would be regarded as complete; and that, for this reason, action on the case could not be postponed."[99]

Thus, despite the fact that one-third or more of the delegates wanted to delay proceedings in order to allow tempers to cool,[100] this "guardian of Presbyterian orthodoxy" forged ahead with determination. Unwilling to accept anything less than an immediate revocation of Briggs's professorship, he railroaded the critical resolution through his committee with a celerity that bore the earmarks of midwestern pressure. The motion read: *"Resolved,* that in the exercise of its right to veto the appointment of professors in the Union Theological Seminary, the General Assembly hereby disapproves of the appointment of Reverend Charles Augustus Briggs to the Edward Robinson Professorship of Biblical Theology in that seminary."[101] Not satisfied that he had succeeded in indicting Briggs, Patton wished to go a step further: motivated by zeal for doctrinal purity, he insisted that a second resolution be entered into the motion. This motion stipulated that a committee of the General Assembly visit Union Seminary as soon as convenient to investigate the New York school on matters of academic sovereignty. The

---

[97] Unmarked and undated newspaper clipping in Hastings, Briggs Scrap Book, I, 71-72.
[98] *Ibid.*
[99] *Ibid.*
[100] *Ibid.*
[101] Clipping of minutes and comments concerning the proceedings of the Detroit General Assembly (1891) in Hastings, Briggs Scrap Book, I, 22-23.

The Charles A. Briggs Heresy Trial

specific question to be investigated was whether the General Assembly or Union had the ultimate power to pass on professors who were transferred from one department to another.[102]

Perfectionist that he was, Patton worked furiously to manipulate the vote on both resolutions. Wavering delegates were buttonholed one by one. To some the political tactics used by this Christian minister from Princeton smacked of Tweed's Tammany Hall.[103] Rev. Frederick J. Pohl, minister of the First Presbyterian Church of Durham, New York, later recalled, "I myself was approached to know how I was going to vote. And when I said that there were no definite charges against Professor Briggs, the man answered with heat and fire that I was the first man that he had met who was voting in favor of Briggs. And then he asked before storming away, 'What presbytery are you from?'"[104]

The Princeton-western alliance not only copied Tammany Hall's pressure methods to win over vacillating eastern delegates, they also pursued Tweed's well-tried practice of exploiting ignorance. Dr. Charles H. Parkhurst, minister-delegate from the Madison Avenue Presbyterian Church of New York City, demonstrated how this method worked. Parkhurst took pains to inquire of many hinterland delegates what they thought higher criticism was. "Their one impression seemed to be that it was a frightful doctrinal disease," reported Parkhurst, "and that Dr. Briggs had it in its most malignant form. The General Assembly were frightened—I had better say panic-stricken. They had no desire to be rid of Union Theological

---

[102] What Patton really had in mind was that if the committee sent to Union from the General Assembly could persuade Union's directorate that full sovereignty lay with the Assembly according to the 1870 Compact, then Union could be effectively controlled relative to higher criticism. The story can be put together by checking "Puzzled over Dr. Briggs," unmarked and undated newspaper clipping in Hastings, Briggs Scrap Book, I, 32; "Hitting Men like Dr. Briggs," unmarked and undated newspaper clipping in Hastings, *ibid.*, I, 72.

[103] "Lights and Shadows of the General Assembly," unmarked and undated newspaper clipping in Hastings, *ibid.*, I, 23.

[104] "A Sheaf of Arrows," New York *Evangelist,* July 9, 1891.

Seminary, but they were afraid of Dr. Briggs, and figured that by exorcizing him, they would save the Seminary by expelling the one evil spirit by which the Seminary seemed possessed."[105]

Where overt pressure failed, still another technique succeeded. The roll-call method of voting, which required each delegate to stand and be counted, was utilized as a coercive device. Hence there was a last-minute scramble into the fold of orthodoxy lest the stragglers themselves be suspected of heresy.[106]

To no one's surprise, therefore, the General Assembly voted to revoke the appointment of Briggs, by the lopsided margin of 440–60.[107] The midwesterners' self-satisfaction, however, was unwarranted, for they really owed their resounding victory to their eastern collaborators, President Francis L. Patton and Dr. William H. Green.

Many delegates suspected that the vote was not a test of pro-higher criticism sentiment in the Presbyterian church.[108] Indeed, not a few commissioners later confessed that they had voted for the resolution against their better judgment. As one journal put it: "It was a Pyrrhic victory. There was not one attempt to applause. No one was happy. Although Union Theological Seminary adherents had met their Waterloo, although the conservatives had won the victory, there was no rejoicing."[109]

The vehement repercussion that came in the weeks and months ahead served to vindicate this paper's verdict. Indeed, such was the din and volume of popular reaction against the General Assembly that it lent credence to a previously published judgment that Briggs was at the head of a great party made up from all

---

[105] "Lights and Shadows of the General Assembly." Perhaps one reason Parkhurst was so conscious of Tammany Hall methods was that he was, besides a minister, a famous anti-Tammany reformer. See Lefferts A. Loetscher, *The Broadening Church* (Philadelphia, 1954), p. 54.

[106] Clipping of minutes and comments concerning the proceedings of the Detroit General Assembly (1891) in Hastings, Briggs Scrap Book, I, 22-23.

[107] *Ibid.*
[108] *Ibid.*
[109] *Ibid.*

branches of Protestantism, and that such was the force of this movement that it was virtually emerging to be a theological reformation whose basis was the new science of higher criticism.[110]

[110] "The Theological Contest."

CHAPTER V

**The Immediate Aftermath of the
Detroit General Assembly: 1891**

The reactions that followed hard on the heels of the Detroit decision were not so much concerned with the larger issue of higher criticism as with the questionable political tactics used against Professor Briggs.

The East was especially vocal. One item that particularly annoyed seaboard ministers and commissioners was the way in which the midwestern presbyteries had fixed the vote by choosing prejudiced delegates. "Briggs never had a chance," complained one New York clergyman, "because more than sixty-two presbyteries had already sat in judgment on the case of Dr. Briggs."[1]

Other maneuvers at Detroit came under attack, especially those resorted to by Princeton divines. Many eastern newspapers were incensed over the bigotry shown by Dr. Patton. His selection as chairman of the committee to prosecute Briggs seemed unjust and highly unethical. If the election of predisposed midwestern delegates promised a victory for the reactionaries, the choice of the Princeton College president guaranteed it.[2] The marriage of convenience between the provincial Midwest and polished Princeton theologians convinced many easterners that the heavy vote against Briggs was

---

[1] "Comments on the General Assembly's Action and Temper," unmarked and undated newspaper clipping in Hastings, Briggs Scrap Book, I, 37-39; "To Whom It May Concern," unmarked newspaper clipping dated June 11, 1891, in Hastings, *ibid.*, I, 24.

[2] "Briggsdoxy: The Union Seminary Should Free Itself from It," unmarked and undated newspaper clipping Hastings, *ibid.*, I, 4.

no true reflection of the sentiment of the majority of delegates. "What we see here," commented an eastern journal, "is a barren triumph of a party rather than a conscientious judgment on higher criticism."[3]

Even parts of the Midwest demonstrated displeasure with some of the things that had gone on in Michigan. Curiously enough, one of the complaints revealed that higher criticism had made an impact upon the intellectuals of even this area. The matter which seemed to bother the hinterland intelligentsia most was that the General Assembly had refused to give reasons for passing judgment against Briggs. Dr. Llewellyn Evans of Lane Seminary contended that he knew why: "The real reasons for not giving any reason," asserted this inland liberal, ". . . were those which a good many leaders of the General Assembly had neither the courage . . . nor candor to avow. Such an avowal would have been in direct conflict with their own claims and professions."[4]

Evans, a cautious Welshman, was not the man to make such an accusation without proof. He knew how both Dr. Francis Brown, successor to Briggs's professorship in Hebrew, and Dr. Willis J. Beecher of Auburn Seminary had provided incontrovertible evidence that even the moderator at Detroit had been influenced by new science.[5] Even Patton, the impeccable inquisitor himself, had made surprising concessions to the heretical trends of the day.[6] If eastern newspapers argued that the Detroit vote did not reflect the genuine convictions of the majority on higher criticism, the discerning Lane professor said the decision demonstrated one thing: the verdict against Briggs showed that many delegates, under pres-

---

[3] "A Contrast: the Assemblies of 1890 and 1891," unmarked and undated newspaper clipping in Hastings, *ibid.*, I, 4.

[4] Llewellyn J. Evans, "No Reasons," unmarked and undated newspaper clipping in Hastings, *ibid.*, I, 21.

[5] Francis Brown, "The Inerrance of Scripture," New York *Evangelist*, July 2, 1891; Willis J. Beecher, "The Situation," unmarked and undated article in Hastings, Briggs Scrap Book, I, 27-28.

[6] "Dr. Patton: A Theological Janus," unmarked and undated newspaper clipping in Hastings, *ibid.*, Vol. III, back cover.

sure of the roll-call vote, had scampered into the orthodox camp to protect their own reputations.[7]

Delayed reactions to the Detroit veto, in contrast to the immediate, revealed much more as to actual sentiment on higher criticism.

Typical of mid- as well as far-western opinion was that of the *Western Christian Advocate*. Briggs's methods and manners were simply too radical. "Young theologians are full enough of speculations and criticism," warned this journal, "without the injection of doubts by their professors."[8]

Even non-typical midwestern sentiment, that is, responses which showed some appreciation for Briggs's point of view, manifested this familiar pattern of hostility. A letter from Madison, Wisconsin, to the editor of the New York *Evangelist* disclosed this ambivalent reaction. Although he evinced some sympathy for certain aspects of higher criticism, the Madisonian concluded with the standard bias: "Biblical criticism is yet very far from being an exact science; and it mars its own best work just in the degree that it puts on the airs of an exact science, and shouts too much before it is out of the woods . . . consequently, Briggs's certainties are no certainties at all; they are simply possibilities, perhaps plausibilities, but nothing more."[9]

It was precisely because higher criticism had so much about it that was plausible that it caused concern among many Bible-believing midwesterners. This apprehension was accurately mirrored when

---

[7] Clipping of minutes and comments concerning the proceedings of the Detroit General Assembly (1891) in Hastings, *ibid.*, I, 22-23; Evans, "No Reasons."

[8] "Points from Pulpit and Press," unmarked and undated newspaper clipping with condensation of press and pulpit reactions to the Detroit Assembly, in Hastings, *ibid.*, I, 54.

[9] "The Higher Criticism: Not an Exact Science," New York *Evangelist*, July 15, 1891. Perhaps Madison, Wisconsin, was more liberal than most of the Midwest because it felt the liberal influence of the University of Wisconsin. Richard T. Ely, for instance, saturated that university with progressive doctrines in economics. He was also influential in the liberalization of Christianity. See his *Social Aspects of Christianity* (New York, 1889).

one paper observed that the issue discussed and decided upon at Detroit was no ephemeral issue. Uneasy as to what might be going on in the minds of theological leaders in its own area, this journal reluctantly admitted that modern views were "avowedly shared by numerous professors in various Presbyterian seminaries as well as by numerous prominent Presbyterian clergymen."[10]

Some of the Midwest's *institutional* allies in the East were frequently more acrimonious in their denunciation of higher criticism than was the Midwest itself. The New York *Mail and Express,* consistently reactionary, attacked the General Assembly for not having gone far enough: the Assembly should have also vetoed the transfer of Dr. Francis Brown to Briggs's vacant chair in Hebrew because "it was known that Brown believed in Briggs as Plato believed in Socrates . . . The Christian Church has no room for the likes of men whose animus is to make out that the Holy Bible is full of errors."[11]

The midwestern view that the Detroit Assembly's action was just and expedient was strengthened by voices within Protestant denominations other than Presbyterian. Baptists throughout the country were natural comrades-in-arms of conservative Presbyterians. Typical Baptist feeling was expressed in one of its leading organs when it remonstrated against all doubt-raising higher critics: "You say you have doubts about this or that, but then there are some things you should have no doubts about. Keep your doubts to yourself, and preach what you know, and you will find that that will take all of your time."[12]

While delayed midwestern reactions were clearly in favor of the Detroit decree, delayed eastern opinions were not. It was the consensus of coastal feeling that Briggs had been dismissed sum-

---

[10] Unmarked and undated newspaper clipping in Hastings, Briggs Scrap Book, I, 71-72.

[11] "Briggs, Brown and Company," newspaper clipping marked and dated New York *Mail and Express,* September 1, 1891, in Hastings, *ibid.,* I, 45-46.

[12] "Points from Pulpit and Press." For an excellent discussion of the anti-intellectual character of right-wing Protestant sects, see Chapter IV, "Evangelicalism and the Revivalists," and Chapter V, "The Revolt against Modernity," in Richard Hofstadter, *Anti-intellectualism in American Life* (New York, 1963), pp. 81-141.

marily and that his contentions had not been granted an intelligent hearing. One easterner wrote that he was "old enough to have become a conservative and to be ranked as reactionary . . . but true conservatism does not lie in that direction taken by the General Assembly concerning Briggs."[13]

Another eastern conservative, from Princeton, attempted to explain why the Detroit verdict was not in the interest of "true conservatism." He asserted that the General Assembly's decision was unwise because it meant that "the Presbyterian Church had decided that, from henceforth, no Presbyterian should look upon . . . the Bible except through the orthodox, Princeton spectacles."[14]

The New York *Tribune* enlarged upon this argument. The Assembly ruling, it stated, signified that right-wing Presbyterians, who were admittedly guardians of their denomination's theology, had turned thumbs down on all intellectual advances resulting from modern biblical scholarship. "The effects of the decision of the veto of Briggs," noted this paper, "will probably turn men's minds away from the Church because it prohibits and punishes every step of advance from its creeds." In contrast to the unprogressive church, the *Tribune* emphasized, the world was making great strides intellectually. But in the church, men were apparently to be told they had no place in its organization unless they exalted its dogmas of faith at the expense of discoveries owing to rational investigation.[15]

The Tribune in its censure of the General Assembly was representative of other enlightened newspapers in the East. The New York *Herald,* for instance, concurred with the *Tribune* and added a few uncomplimentary remarks of its own. In censorious tone the *Herald* wondered why the Assembly had stopped with Briggs: why had it not gone right ahead and condemned a whole host of Presbyterian leaders who shared the Union professor's heretical beliefs?[16]

Seaboard religious journals likewise expressed sympathy for

---
[13] "A Sheaf of Arrows," New York *Evangelist,* July 9, 1891.
[14] *Ibid.*
[15] "One More Heretic," New York *Tribune,* May 31, 1891.
[16] Undated clipping from the New York *Herald* in Hastings, Briggs Scrap Book, I, 22.

Briggs. The New York *Evangelist,* a leading Presbyterian organ, was especially outspoken. Although unhappy with the immediate results of the Detroit Assembly, the *Evangelist* noted that the conclave had accomplished at least one thing for higher criticism: it had publicized the new critical views both within and without the church. This New York paper correctly grasped something else about the effects of the Detroit gathering: it predicted that the Assembly's proceedings were merely the first encounter of a battle that would go on indefinitely.[17]

While eastern *institutions* supported the Midwest, *individuals* scattered throughout the Mississippi and Ohio valley regions upheld seaboard Presbyterians in a critical evaluation of the Detroit veto. Dr. Hamilton, a leading St. Louis pastor, was one of these brave souls. Jeopardizing his position because of local hostility to modernism, Hamilton asserted, "Thoughtful men are saying . . . that our Church will not allow her scholars to make a thorough study of the Bible by the modern scientific methods unless they first bind themselves to no conclusions save such as are acceptable to a certain theological school in the Church." This struck the St. Louis minister as particularly "calamitous" because it was driving intellectuals out of the Presbyterian denomination.[18] Hamilton was not opposed to allowing Briggs to continue in the service of the Presbyterian church so long as he endorsed the essentials of the faith.

Still another midwesterner, Dr. Herrick Johnson of McCormick Seminary in Chicago, demonstrated unusual courage when he contended there was no question that Briggs was "evangelical." Johnson's plea in behalf of the Union scholar is of especial value because he showed that the entire "evangelical spectrum" had felt the impact of higher criticism. Johnson began by saying that the Detroit General Assembly had really misunderstood Briggs's position. There were two kinds of higher critics, as different from each other as day from night. He categorized them as "rational" and "evangelical."

---

[17] "The Storm Center at Detroit," New York *Evangelist,* June 4, 1891.

[18] "Dr. Hamilton on Professor Briggs," unmarked and undated newspaper clipping in Hastings, Briggs Scrap Book, I, 24.

The Charles A. Briggs Heresy Trial

Johnson felt obligated to explain his startling contrast. "Think of the confusion which would reign," he said, "if we confused the Christian evolutionists like Asa Gray with the atheistic evolutionists. But that is exactly what the General Assembly has done with Briggs, except in the realm of Higher Criticism." Such a distinction was valid because both the Christian higher critic and the Christian evolutionist maintained a deep respect for the Holy Scriptures. Johnson explained further:

> The rational Higher Critics flatly deny the divine authority of the Bible. The evangelical Critics accept that authority. The rational Critics repudiate the supernatural. The evangelical Critics believe in the supernatural. The rational Critics tear the Bible to pieces and so scatter its leaves up and down the centuries as to make an utter jumble of Biblical history. The evangelical Critics give Biblical history a unique importance.[19]

After drawing these contrasts, Johnson asked rhetorically which of these schools Briggs belonged to. He boldly asserted there could be no doubt that Briggs belonged to the evangelical higher critics because of his belief in both the Holy Scriptures and modern scholarship. He concluded his penetrating observations on the Detroit veto by noting, "When therefore in his Inaugural Address Briggs spoke of 'The Critics' as the victorious army confronting the Bible, he was clearly not referring to the rational Critics like Kuenen and Wellhausen, but to the evangelical Critics."[20]

Johnson's article, by way of implication, showed that in attempting to modify American theology, Charles A. Briggs was like Richard T. Ely in economics, Lester F. Ward in sociology, and William James in psychology. None of these other three men sought to uproot any phase of the American heritage. Each in his own sphere endeavored to modernize his particular discipline. Through German ideas in economics, sociology, and psychology, these three men helped to modify the older American pattern of

---
[19] Herrick Johnson, "Confounding Things that Differ," unmarked and undated newspaper clipping in Hastings, *ibid.*, I, 25-26.
[20] *Ibid.*

laissez faire with the pattern of social cooperation. Rationalism in all three cases was the basis of these concerted experiments.

German rationalism was likewise the means of renovating American theology. Like its sister disciplines, American theology, which had long been comparatively indifferent to *this* world, was related meaningfully to the problems of this side of paradise. One result was the rise of the Social Gospel with its emphasis upon rectification of this world's injustices.

Taken in this sense, Briggs's task was similar to the tasks of Ely, Ward, and James. Although accepting the basic premises of German thought, each man had to so modify German suppositions as to make them palatable to American traditions.[21] The interesting parallel can be carried a step further: each man was judged a heretic in his own day, but each was vindicated by the turn of subsequent events.

Although the general public reaction to the Detroit General Assembly revealed much as to the theological revolution in the 1890's, action taken within the walls of Union Theological Seminary relative to the Detroit decision made it clear that the new approach to the Bible had been all but completely accepted by the avantgarde of religious thinkers.

---

[21] A good discussion on how nineteenth-century scholars were adapting these new ideas to American traditions can be found in Chapter 2, "Intellectual Tides," George E. Mowry, *The Era of Theodore Roosevelt* (New York, 1958), pp. 16-37.

CHAPTER VI

Official Reaction to the Detroit General Assembly: Summer-Fall, 1891

It was inevitable that Union Theological Seminary would have to choose whether to accept or reject the verdict reached at Detroit. Briggs, however, had forced his school to make the choice at a most inauspicious time. While Princeton Seminary had more students, Union was in 1891 the most highly endowed of all Presbyterian seminaries. Some members of the directorate thought that in order to retain this affluent position, nothing should be done to offend its Presbyterian benefactors. Considerations of finance dictated that the heretical professor must go.

The way, however, in which Union would react to the Detroit verdict had been accurately predicted at the time of the Assembly by Dr. Schaff, the seminary's church historian. To a direct question, Schaff replied that there was little doubt in his mind that Union would defend Briggs and his teachings to the very end.[1] This prediction was corroborated by another Union faculty member, Dr. Francis Brown, who promptly promised, "Now we will become militant in our efforts to promote Higher Criticism and stand by Briggs."[2] Unlike outsiders, these two professors knew their school and their colleagues; most of the faculty and board were very sympathetic to liberal theology.[3]

---

[1] Clipping of minutes and comments concerning the proceedings of the Detroit General Assembly (1891) in Hastings, Briggs Scrap Book, I, 22-23.

[2] Undated clipping from the New York *Herald* in Hastings, *ibid.*, I, 2.

[3] "The Briggs Case and the Board of Education," New York *Evangelist*, October 29, 1891, in Hastings, *ibid.*, I, 72; "The Conference," undated clipping from the Cincinnati *Herald and Presbyter* in Hastings, *ibid.*, I, 33;

If Schaff and Brown were prepared for Union's official response to Detroit, many Presbyterians (especially in the Midwest) were shocked and scandalized when on June 9, 1891, the directors of the New York school publicly announced that the board had voted to defy the General Assembly's veto of Brigg's professorship. This action struck many of the orthodox as a defense not only of the heretic's academic position but also of his teachings.[4]

The executive board had not made its critical decision without due deliberation. The Union policy makers realized that the first legal argument they had chosen to defend their position was flimsy: they claimed that if Detroit could make an *ex parte* decision, so could Union.[5] Hence, to protect themselves from possible criticism, the directors abandoned this argument and turned to a much stronger legal argument, derived from the ambiguities of the terms of the Compact of 1870. This defiant action was founded upon stipulations in the 1870 agreement that the General Assembly could pass only on elections, and not on transfers, of the seminary's professors.[6] "Internal transfers," argued the directorate, were strictly the business of local administrators. Basing its legal defense on this "transfer stipulation," Union insisted upon its rights and refused to acquiesce in the Detroit decision.

Union officials fully expected a wave of outside criticism. But censure coming from within its own ranks caught the pro-Briggs group momentarily unprepared. The two directors voting against Union's defiance of the General Assembly made caustic statements to the press. One of them, a Mr. Hall, even resigned in protest.[7] The harshest stricture came from the other dissenting director,

---

"Lights and Shadows of the General Assembly," unmarked and undated newspaper clipping in Hastings, *ibid.*, I, 23.

[4] "Professor Briggs is Sustained by Union," New York *Sun,* June 6, 1891.

[5] *Ibid.*

[6] *Ibid.*

[7] "Union Seminary's Loss," New York *World,* October 18, 1891, in Hastings, Briggs Scrap Book, III, 11. Hall was especially antagonistic towards higher criticism because his son, a Chicago minister, was an enthusiastic follower of Briggs.

The Charles A. Briggs Heresy Trial

R. R. Booth, who charged that the seminary's action had been too "hasty" and "hot-headed."[8]

Nonetheless, Henry Day, the institution's legal adviser, was able to handle the contretemps. He argued that Booth's charges were simply not true. The decision had not been hasty, because it had been considered for months. "If anybody has acted in haste, it was the General Assembly in deciding it could pass on a transfer rather than election."[9]

While Booth charged Union with precipitate action, the New York *Tribune* suggested that the true motive of the directors might have been revenge. This paper noted that the Union directorate had not forgotten how its request for a pre–General Assembly conference had been rebuffed. The New York seminary had wanted to talk over such delicate matters as local sovereignty, transfers, and Briggs's teachings "in camera." But Patton and his allies had shut this door in Union's face. Piqued at such treatment, Union, so many thought, was now seeking revenge.[10]

Actually, neither the manner nor the motive of Union's refusal touched the core of things. What did matter was the way in which the seminary's defiance was interpreted by the enemies of higher criticism. As so often in history, it was not so much what might really have happened as what people thought had happened that mattered. Union's defiance was taken to mean that the seminary was determined to propagate the German theology.

Perhaps such an interpretation by the Midwest was not wholly unwarranted. The New York *World* saw Union's decision to defy the General Assembly as a triumph for both Briggs and higher criticism.[11] To the *World* it seemed that this crisis of conflicting

---

[8] Unmarked and undated newspaper clipping in Hastings, *ibid.*, I, 20.

[9] "The Presbyterian Controversy," unmarked and undated newspaper clipping in Hastings, *ibid.*, I, 22.

[10] "Should They Have Waited?" undated clipping from the New York *Tribune* in Hastings, *ibid.*, II, 9.

[11] "Briggs Triumph," undated clipping from the New York *World* in Hastings, *ibid.*, I, 19-20.

wills had turned the New York seminary, almost overnight, into the chief citadel of the new theology in the United States.[12]

The New York *Times* concurred in this judgment and added a few speculations of its own. Taking note of how the intellectual world was in the midst of a revolution that was overturning absolute standards, the *Times* urged Union, which it deemed the leading liberal seminary in America, to apply the pragmatic principles of this revolution to fields other than higher criticism. It recommended that Union expand its national emphasis to comprehend such subjects as sociology. In short, Union should not stop at establishing a department of higher criticism, but go on to found a department of "Applied Christian Sociology." New York City, concluded the *Times,* would make an ideal laboratory for such a venture because of its teeming slums.[13]

Orthodox Presbyterians, by now in possession of sufficient evidence that Union had been beguiled by the German theologians, laid plans to discipline the rebellious school. With clairvoyant perception, an eastern paper predicted that the midwestern presbyteries would resort to the instrument of boycott.[14]

There was not too much surprise back east, therefore, when the Cincinnati presbytery assumed the leadership of a boycott aimed at preventing ministerial candidates from matriculating at Union. The bellicose Ohioans also exhorted the General Assembly to activate the special committee it had created at Detroit in order to meet with Union as soon as possible. Cincinnati conservatives hoped that this committee would be able to coerce Union back into the orthodox fold. When this was accomplished, Cincinnati could lead a movement to rebuild traditionalism all over America.[15]

Most Bible Belt presbyteries were quick to respond to Cincinnati's call to boycott the institutional nerve center of higher criticism. No ministerial candidate from the Midwest was to matriculate at

---

[12] *Ibid.*

[13] "What Union Seminary Might Do," undated clipping from the New York *Times* in Hastings, Briggs Scrap Book, I, 55.

[14] "Dr. Briggs There to Stay," New York *Sun,* June 6, 1891.

[15] "Cincinnati Presbytery," unmarked and undated newspaper clipping in Hastings, Briggs Scrap Book, III, 5.

The Charles A. Briggs Heresy Trial

Union Seminary. If any prospective divinity student chose to defy his presbytery, he would have to suffer the consequences.

In this movement Union was denounced as a center of heresy, while mid- and far-western seminaries were depicted as examples of doctrinal purity. Inland Presbyterianism was particularly proud that higher criticism had not entered the portals of its seminaries.[16] The Presbyterian schools at Omaha, Chicago, and San Francisco were objects of special praise. These untarnished institutions, exulted one midwestern paper, had successfully withstood the incursions of higher criticism.[17]

Midwestern pressure was also applied indirectly to Union through memorials sent to the General Assembly concerning scholarships. As a result it was decided that the Assembly's Board of Education scholarships would no longer be extended to students planning to enter the New York seminary.[18] However, this plan to coerce students into not going to the Gotham institution failed. Wealthy New York City businessmen created a scholarship fund of their own for entering Union students which more than compensated for the loss of the Assembly's subsidy.[19]

In the end even the boycott movement miscarried. Having gained recognition as one of the most liberal and scholarly institutions in the East, Union began to attract many students from denominations other than Presbyterian. This was particularly true of liberal-minded ministerial candidates from New England, who previously were attracted to either Harvard's or Yale's divinity school.[20]

The Cincinnatians were naturally reluctant to admit defeat. But they were forced eventually to retire to their provincial lairs and contemplate their failure. Rev. S. S. Potter, member of the Cincinnati presbytery, faced the situation realistically. In a speech delivered before the Ministers' Association of his presbytery, he con-

---

[16] "The Orthodoxy of the Church North," undated clipping from the San Francisco *Occident* in Hastings, *ibid.*, III, 29-30.
[17] *Ibid.*
[18] "The Briggs Case and the Board of Education."
[19] *Ibid.*
[20] New York *Tribune,* November 4, 1891.

ceded that the movement to deprive Union of students had been successfully blocked by New England. "There probably would be no diminution of students at Union," he remarked, "because of liberal New England . . . which will now send even more students to Union because of the new views which will be taught there now with even greater intensity."[21]

By midsummer of 1891 sentiment throughout the Midwest reflected Cincinnati's frustration. Union was the momentary victor in this East-West battle over higher criticism.

For the rest of the summer things remained static. Union continued adamant; Cincinnati nursed thoughts of revenge. It was a time for both sides to draw back and contemplate future moves. Moreover, summers in the Protestant calendar are customarily given over to a relaxed church program. Biblical literalists to the end, most of the Cincinnati ministers took to heart the injunction in Ecclesiastes which advised that there is "a time for war, and a time for peace." Accordingly, most spent the hot summer months at one of the pleasant lakes far removed from "Porkopolis."[22] Eastern leaders also fled the muggy weather of New York City. Union closed for the summer, and many of its professors and board members disappeared to favorite vacation spots. Briggs himself took ship for England, there to spend the summer with the famous British higher critic Dr. Samuel R. Driver, in order to complete their famous Hebrew lexicon.[23]

By September, with the sultry season over and ministers back in their pulpits, the drive to discipline Union was renewed. By fall, however, because the General Assembly had authorized its special committee to look into matters at New York, the leadership in this campaign passed from Cincinnati to Princeton in the person of President Patton, who was named chairman of the investigating

---

[21] "The Briggs Controversy," unmarked and undated newspaper clipping in Hastings, Briggs Scrap Book, I, 62-63. The Midwest blamed New England more than any other area in the East for the liberal trend. See "The Briggs Case," New York *Evening Post,* November 5, 1891, in Hastings, *ibid.,* II, 52.

[22] Clipping of minutes and comments concerning the proceedings of the Detroit General Assembly (1891) in Hastings, *ibid.,* I, 22-23.

[23] *Ibid.*

deputation. Patton and his Committee on Conference were instructed to parley with the seminary's executive board on the subject of sovereignty.[24]

Patton, however, had his own ideas as to what the true objective of this mission should be. To be sure, he would obey his directive and discuss the subject of sovereignty; but he planned to use the discussions on control to achieve additional ends. If he could persuade Union that the 1870 Compact stipulated that the General Assembly possessed sovereignty in all things pertaining to seminaries under the Presbyterian church,[25] he would then have the legal means for rooting out the heresy which had long been festering at Union.[26] If this could be achieved in New York, then the rest of the nation would be protected from liberalism. Such was the hope that impelled Patton to go to Union Seminary.

The Princeton president's optimism was unwarranted. Union had neither forgotten nor forgiven Patton for the way he had harassed Briggs at Detroit. Although the Committee on Conference was recognized as legal, New Yorkers regarded it as little more than a midwestern front. Patton, as he had been at the Detroit Assembly, was regarded as a mouthpiece for the hinterland.[27] Moreover, the executive board at Union regarded the Committee on Conference an open affront.[28] The Union managers had wanted to resolve differences in a less conspicuous way but had been denied this privilege.[29] Rebuffed at every turn, Union was now to be subjected to additional injury by an investigation.

When Patton and his committee entered the Union campus in late October, they were met with cool defiance.[30] The Princetonian made the New York school's board feel as if they were being subjected to an inquisition instituted by its rival, Princeton Seminary,

---

[24] "Briggs and his Professorship," unmarked and undated newspaper clipping in Hastings, Briggs Scrap Book, I, 30.
[25] *Ibid.*
[26] *Ibid.*
[27] *Ibid.*
[28] "The Storm Center at Detroit," New York *Evangelist,* June 4, 1891.
[29] *Ibid.*
[30] *Ibid.*

rather than by the General Assembly.[31] Patton's problems increased when it was discovered that the directors of Union had been at work all summer preparing an adequate defense based on the "transfer argument."[32]

It was a foregone conclusion that Patton would fail at Union; to no one's surprise the two-day session between Union and the Patton committee ended in a stalemate.[33] Patton would not take less than full sovereignty for the General Assembly; Union's policy makers refused to relinquish the power to make transfers.[34] One of Union's most convincing arguments was that the ambiguity of the 1870 Compact could be cleared up by asking the surviving members of the directorate who had drawn up that agreement what really had been stipulated. To a man, the surviving members maintained that the 1870 settlement had granted the General Assembly power to pass only on elections, and not on transfers, of professors in Union Seminary.[35] The impasse between the New York school and the General Assembly stood in October just where it had in June.

In assessing the meaning of the stalemate, most papers failed to see the larger issue at stake and became absorbed in the legal complexities of the proceedings. But the center of midwestern hostility towards higher criticism appraised the real issue. Cincinnati's *Herald and Presbyter,* owned by two of the most reactionary members of the local presbytery, correctly held the deadlock a victory for higher criticism.[36] The crucial question, said the Ohio journal, was not sovereignty but German theology. The essence of the

---

[31] Patton was a midwesterner at heart. Brilliant professor of theology at McCormick Seminary and editor of the Chicago *Interior,* he had as early as the mid-1870s earned a reputation as a heresy hunter. See Lefferts Loetscher, *The Broadening Church* (Philadelphia, 1954), pp. 12-14.

[32] "That Briggs Conference," unmarked newspaper clipping dated October 29, 1891, in Hastings, Briggs Scrap Book, I, 29.

[33] "Union Seminary's Standing," New York *Evening Post,* October 30, 1891.

[34] "Puzzled Over Dr. Briggs," unmarked and undated newspaper clipping in Hastings, Briggs Scrap Book, I, 32.

[35] "Union Stands by Briggs," New York *Times,* October 30, 1891.

[36] "The Conference."

The Charles A. Briggs Heresy Trial 83

struggle, it asserted, was whether critical theories would be allowed or suppressed in Presbyterian seminaries. Patton's failure to budge Union meant only one thing: Presbyterian liberals had won another round. But Union's inflexibility also signified something else—that the New York school was committed to a general campaign to conquer the country for higher criticism.[37]

There were other reasons why Union Seminary remained steadfast. Gotham's Presbyterians were prompted partly by revenge. The seminary's managers did not forget that the General Assembly had broken its promise not to prosecute Briggs if the New York school secured assurances of his orthodoxy.[38] Furthermore, Union men were unable to dismiss from their memories how Union had been snubbed at Detroit relative to representation on key committees which dealt with the higher criticism matter.[39] In addition, Union for obvious reasons wished to retain as far as possible the local autonomy it had enjoyed before the Compact of 1870.

Constitutional and personal motives notwithstanding, there was little denying the appraisal of the Cincinnati *Herald and Presbyter*. Union had mapped its future carefully; it would henceforth function as a hub for the dissemination of liberal theology. This plan was facilitated by the retirement of the last of the old-school theologians, Dr. Shedd, from the faculty.[40] Union now had a faculty that was overwhelmingly behind Briggs, and the school was completely ready to do what it could to liberalize American theology.

Union's unanimity on biblical criticism provided another motive for defying the Patton committee. If full sovereignty were granted the General Assembly, it would have the power to remove not only Briggs but the whole Union faculty for heretical convictions. Union's obstinacy, therefore, is explained by a complex of interrelated factors, chief of which was a defense of German theology.

The Patton committee's meeting with Union in October marked the high tide of the Detroit assault against Briggs. Patton's failure

---
[37] *Ibid.*
[38] "Union Stands by Briggs."
[39] Clipping of minutes and comments concerning the proceedings of the Detroit General Assembly (1891) in Hastings, Briggs Scrap Book, I, 22-23.
[40] "The Conference."

at the New York seminary symbolized the beginning of the end for the present attack. But if the orthodox of the East had given up, their midwestern colleagues had not surrendered. Accordingly, the leadership of the anti-Briggs campaign passed once more into the hands of Cincinnati. Before the meeting of Patton's committee with Union, many midwestern presbyteries wished to follow a policy of watchful waiting, hoping all the time for some compromise. But the ensuing impasse vindicated Cincinnati's fears; as a result midwestern presbyteries turned again to the councils of southern Ohio Presbyterians for further guidance.[41]

Although the Cincinnati purists possessed zeal, they sometimes lacked imagination. The only plan they could now devise was the familiar tactic of boycott.[42] Since no other presbytery could propose anything better, the Cincinnati recommendation was pursued with the fanaticism of champions of a losing cause. Typical midwestern cooperation was the action of the presbytery of Freeport, Illinois. "At the . . . fall meeting of the Freeport Presbytery," recorded Rev. Samuel C. Haig, a member of that body, "our members unanimously disapproved of young men going to Union Theological Seminary for their ministerial training so long as it persists in championing higher criticism and Briggs."[43] Bible-loving Presbyterians in rural Pennsylvania were just as fervent in their resolutions.[44] The upper South, especially Maryland and Virginia, also joined in the move against Union. The presbytery of Washington City, Virginia, was the most articulate, it absolutely forbade ministerial students to set foot on Union's campus.[45]

Personal reactions to Union's defiance were sometimes more heated than were presbyterial. This was particularly so within the border states, a region that was fast becoming an ally of the Mid-

---

[41] "Union's Loss, Princeton's Gain," New York *Sun*, December 30, 1891.

[42] "Cincinnati: Theological Instructors Warned," Philadelphia *Presbyterian*, December 30, 1891.

[43] "Doesn't Believe in Briggs, Brown and Company," unmarked and undated newspaper clipping in Hastings, Briggs Scrap Book, I, 47.

[44] "Presbytery of Lehigh—Its Relation to Union Theological Seminary," Lehigh *Register*, September 30, 1891, in Hastings, *ibid.*, I, 49-50.

[45] "Union's Loss, Princeton's Gain."

west. One of the most dramatic personal measures taken against Union was that of John T. De Sellum of Rockville, Maryland. De Sellum had planned to will his entire modest estate to Union. Following Union's defiance of Patton's committee, he changed his will and made Princeton Seminary his sole beneficiary. De Sellum was of no mind to see his money subsidize heresy; his estate would help the gospel or nothing.[46]

By the end of November, 1891, it was clear that Union had been unaffected by the Midwest's stratagem. If anything, Union had more students than ever. Cincinnati had failed to contain higher criticism by declaring the eastern theological institutions unsafe.

Frustrated in its attempt to suppress higher criticism in Union Seminary by Patton's committee or by boycott, the Midwest was left only one alternative: bitter criticism of the East and passionate self-praise. "There is a great deal going on . . . that from a western and southern point of view is fearfully off color," fulminated one paper from the Southwest. There was much that the East tolerated that scandalized the West. "Somehow," exclaimed one paper in an attempt to defend hinterland intransigence, "heresy doesn't seem to scare them [the East] as much as it does us."[47]

Mid- and far-westerners gloried that their schools of theological learning were citadels of doctrinal purity. McCormick Seminary in Chicago, backed by money made from reapers whose name it bore, was held up as the Princeton of the West.[48] The self-praise continued concerning other faithful institutions in Nebraska and California.[49] The East and North, exulted one journal, had their admitted heretics, but the whole of the West and South stood immovably for othodoxy.[50]

The Cincinnati-engineered campaign to silence Briggs failed in its larger aims but had indirect results. The drive demonstrated how deeply German theology had cut into American intellectual circles. In particular, it showed that the point of greatest penetration was

---

[46] *Ibid.*
[47] "The Orthodoxy of the Church North."
[48] *Ibid.*
[49] *Ibid.*
[50] *Ibid.*

the East.[51] But there were signs that metropolitan centers all over the land were beginning to feel the effect of the new theology. The advance of higher criticism into the Midwest, however, is more clearly detectable in the second official counteroffensive of the Presbyterian church against the heretical Union professor.[52]

By late September, Patton, like many other conservatives, sensed that the General Assembly movement against Briggs was weakening. The last Assembly effort, the conference between Union and the Patton committee, had resulted in an impasse. Briggs, however, was still talking and writing; he had to be stopped.

Such reasoning must account for the further maneuvers of Dr. Patton. He devoted less and less time to the General Assembly movement, but gave his energies increasingly to the second official thrust of the Presbyterian church against Briggs: the New York City presbytery's heresy trial.[53]

To this anachronistic inquest attention must now be given.

---

[51] "In his own Defense," New York *World,* May 6, 1891; "Briggs's Champions," New York *World,* May 31, 1891; "Dr. Stevens on Inspiration," New York *World,* May 31, 1891.

[52] Lane Seminary was an influence for liberal theology in the Midwest. But the conservatives of Cincinnati succeeded in forcing it into the orthodox mold by 1900. See Lefferts Loetscher, *The Broadening Church* (Philadelphia, 1954), p. 66. At the same time a liberal journal whose purpose was to disseminate higher criticism was in the process of being established in Cleveland, *ca.* 1892. See "The New Religion," Philadelphia *Presbyterian,* January 6, 1892.

[53] "Will Stand by Dr. Briggs," unmarked and undated newspaper clipping in Hastings, Briggs Scrap Book, I, 29.

CHAPTER VII

**The New York City Presbytery—
Initial Proceedings in the Briggs Case: April, 1891**

The second official assault of the Presbyterian church against Briggs, though differing in result, was similar in origin. Like the Detroit Assembly's thrust, the attack of the New York City presbytery received its first impetus from midwestern pressure. Had this pressure not been applied, it is doubtful whether Gotham would have been treated to, and embarrassed by, the spectacle of a modern heresy trial.

To this point in the present study, midwestern hostility to liberal theology has been described rather than analyzed. Inasmuch as it had so much to do with the entire Briggs affair, an analysis of that antipathy is warranted at this juncture.

The Midwest's abhorrence of theological innovation had deep historical roots. For Briggs was not the first victim of that region's bigotry. From the days of Thomas Jefferson, the Presbyterian church had been rocked by periodic heresy trials instigated by the puritanical Midwest. In almost every instance the hinterland's bellicosity was directed as much against the East as against any particular heretic.

For instance, in the 1830's there was the heresy trial of Lyman Beecher, president of Lane Seminary, over the doctrine of the Trinity, an inquisition begun and carried through by midwesterners. In striking parallel to the Briggs case, chief opposition to Beecher stemmed from the presbytery of Cincinnati, which was even then determined that liberal theology would not cross the Alleghenies.[1]

---
[1] Philip Schaff, "Other Heresy Trials and the Briggs Case," unmarked and undated article in Hastings, Briggs Scrap Book, III, 5-6.

A few years later came the trial of Albert Barnes, who, like Beecher, was accused of having imbibed his unorthodox beliefs from New England liberalism.[2] One of the most celebrated events in the annals of American Presbyterianism, the Barnes trial rent the Presbyterian church asunder. The East-West schism was not healed until after the Civil War. Although legally reconciled in 1870,[3] the two wings of the denomination vividly remembered the Barnes episode. The scars of the thirty-year rift were still discernible in 1891, the year in which Briggs's inaugural reopened old wounds.

The Midwest's theological provincialism also drew its strength from intellectual isolationism. Although calumny had pervaded the heresy trials of Andrew Jackson's day, the invective was much more abusive in Briggs's case. This difference in intensity of feeling can be partly explained by the respective origins of the heresies. Whereas the unorthodox views of Beecher and Barnes had sprung from American soil,[4] Briggs's doctrine was a foreign importation. Midwesterners, intellectual as well as political isolationists, sharply recoiled from higher criticism because it was a European heresy sullying the purity of American Protestantism.[5] Taken in this sense, the trans-Allegheny enmity towards Briggs as the chief apostle of German theology can be regarded as a late-nineteenth-century revival of Know Nothingism. In one respect this recoil was an even more radical form of bigotry than that of the 1850's. Then, it was Protestant against Catholic; now, it was reactionary Protestant against liberal Protestant.[6]

Finally, the vehemence with which the Midwest pounced upon Briggs had theological implications. To be sure, Briggs's exasperating public demeanor antagonized eastern Protestants as well as western.[7] But the Midwest's intensified hostility towards the doc-

---

[2] *Ibid.*
[3] *Ibid.*
[4] *Ibid.*
[5] For a penetrating analysis of midwestern isolationism, see Selig Adler, *The Isolationist Impulse* (New York, 1957), pp. 43-45.
[6] Schaff, "Other Heresy Trials and the Briggs Case."
[7] *Ibid.*

The Charles A. Briggs Heresy Trial

trine of the New York scholar was much more deeply rooted, for the Bible Belt feared Briggs's influence on his students. One alumnus testified that while Shedd had left him cold, with an icy stress upon "tradition, tradition, tradition," Briggs had so stimulated him that, he said, "I owe more to Dr. Briggs than anyone else."[8] What horrified the faithful of the Ohio Valley region still more was the spell that Briggs cast over students training to be missionaries. This influence was clearly demonstrated when a former student, now a missionary to the Orient, wrote home, "I defy any man to prove the infallibility of the Bible. For my part, I do not see how a revelation given to men could be infallible."[9] Recognized as the leading exponent of higher criticism in America for a full decade,[10] Briggs seemed to the West bent on an unrelenting program to undermine the very cornerstone of historic Protestantism, the Bible.[11]

The Midwest's fear of Briggs was not limited to his classroom utterances; his prolific publications caused an even greater scare.[12] His classroom lectures influenced future ministers, but his publications were a potent force on the laity. Briggs, it will be recalled, had returned from his *Wanderjahre* determined to modernize American theology through higher criticism.[13] Realizing that he was limited in both classroom and public forum because of his denomination's stand, he turned to the printed page as an avenue of expression. Despite a heavy teaching load and an outside lecturing schedule,[14] he found the time and energy to write many books, articles, and

---

[8] New York *Evangelist*, June 25, 1891.

[9] "How It Looks to a Missionary," undated clipping from the New York *Evangelist* in Hastings, Briggs Scrap Book, I, 14.

[10] "Dr. Briggs and Revision," New York *Tribune*, October 5, 1891.

[11] "Commentary on the Briggs Case," San Francisco *Occident*, November 25, 1891, in Hastings, Briggs Scrap Book, Vol. II, inside front cover.

[12] "Dr. Briggs at Close Range," undated clipping from the New York *World* in Hastings, *ibid.*, I, 53-54.

[13] Briggs to Henry Boynton Smith, May 6, 1868, in Emilie Grace Briggs, Letters, III, 461-465.

[14] Unmarked and undated newspaper clipping in Hastings, Briggs Scrap Book, I, 40-41; "New York: Biblical Theology," unmarked and undated newspaper clipping in Hastings, *ibid.*, I, 74.

pamphlets all aimed at disseminating the new theology.[15] He was greatly aided in this effort by his devoted daughter, Emilie Grace Briggs, who mastered Hebrew in order to assist him. Had it not been for Emilie, Briggs probably never would have been so prolific in writing.[16]

Easterners, aware of midwestern hostility towards theological change, were not surprised when it was discovered that the hinterland Presbyterians were attempting to put pressure on the New York presbytery to try Briggs for heresy. But if the pressure itself was expected, the way in which it was applied was particularly galling. Midwesterners made it crystal-clear that failure to act would be regarded as proof that the New York presbytery itself had fallen prey to heterodox German ideas. Once more the presbytery of Cincinnati emerged as the motivating center in this new movement to halt Briggs and religious liberalism.[17]

Although incensed at this meddling, the New York presbytery feared to give the Cincinnati reactionaries grounds for believing that their accusation was correct. To keep the presbytery's reputation spotless, members of that body reluctantly decided to institute action against Briggs.[18] On April 13, 1891, the presbytery created

---

[15] The titles of some of Briggs's works are enough to suggest what they contain: *Address on Exegetical Theology* (1876); *The Rights, Duty, Limits of Biblical Criticism* (1881); *Biblical Study: Its Methods and History* (1883); *Study of Higher Criticism with Special Reference to the Pentateuch* (1883); *Messianic Prophecy* (1886); *Whither?* (1889).

[16] "Dr. Briggs at Close Range."

[17] "Turn Him Out," undated clipping from the New York *Mail and Express* in Hastings, Briggs Scrap Book, III, 15; clipping from the Pittsburgh *Banner*, December 30, 1891, in Hastings, *ibid.*, III, 2; "Cincinnati Presbytery," unmarked and undated newspaper clipping in Hastings, *ibid.*, III, 5.

[18] "Turn Him Out." Midwestern and upper southern presbyteries from Iowa to Virginia took their cue from Cincinnati. See "Still Another Overture," unmarked newspaper clipping dated May 9, 1891, in Hastings, Briggs Scrap Book, III, 16; "To Sever Union Seminary," unmarked and undated newspaper clippings in Hastings, *ibid.*, III, 19.

The Charles A. Briggs Heresy Trial

a committee of inquiry and instructed it to investigate whether Briggs should stand trial.[19]

This decision, however, came not only as a result of lobbying from southern Ohio. Within New York's liberal presbytery there existed a hard core of militant conservatives who increasingly became alarmed at the impact Briggs was making upon the orthodox community. Because they were near the center of the storm brewing at Union, the New York City die-hards knew better than most people the inroads that higher criticism had made in the east.[20] Moreover, they were apprehensive of the influence that Briggs was having upon the minds of young men in the metropolis.[21] Their apprehension turned to alarm with the realization that higher criticism was beginning to make a similar impact upon surrounding states.[22] The sense of disquiet increased further when it was seen that the "theology of doubt" was starting to affect the thinking of certain of the laity.[23]

Nevertheless, this minority was reluctant to institute proceedings against Briggs. Although its numbers encompassed "a considerable group of clergy and laity,"[24] the conservative coterie was realistic enough to see that they would have to confront a pro-Briggs majority. But fear of Briggs's doctrines grew daily. By April all that was needed to ensure action was some outside encouragement. Midwestern warnings were sufficient to prod the orthodox party into action.

Thus, just as the Ohio Valley conservatives had possessed a

---

[19] "Dr. Briggs and his Friends," unmarked and undated newspaper clipping in which the minutes of the April 13 presbytery meeting are recorded, in Hastings, *ibid.*, II, 65.

[20] "Dr. Briggs and Revision," New York *Tribune,* October 5, 1891, in Hastings, *ibid.*, I, 34; "Fearless of Criticism," undated clipping from the New York *Tribune* in Hastings, *ibid.*, I, 18.

[21] "Is Professor Briggs A Heretic?" New York *Sun,* April 12, 1891.

[22] *Ibid.*

[23] *Ibid.*

[24] *Ibid.*

strong eastern ally in Princeton in the Detroit attack against Briggs, so they now had an eastern ally in the conservative minority in the presbytery's move against Briggs. But unlike Patton with his irritating techniques in Michigan, New York traditionalists were forced to exercise restraint because of the ever-present threat of the liberal majority in the presbytery.[25]

An examination of the leadership of the conservative minority is instructive for shedding light on the mentality of easterners fearful of German theology. Midwestern enemies of higher criticism frequently came from the agrarian class; it was different in the East.

The nucleus of this conservative minority was the five-man committee of inquiry created on April 13 to investigate the Briggs matter. Later transformed *de facto* into the Committee of Prosecution, this group was destined to hound the Union teacher until finally, in 1893, he was excommunicated from the Presbyterian church.[26]

The leader of this group was Dr. George W. F. Birch, pastor of Bethany Church of New York City. Birch, a heavy-set man, seemed somehow to be able to communicate a wiry sense of energy; and though he is said to have been a warm human being, he frequently gave the opposite impression. This hard-hitting and occasionally brilliant Presbyterian pastor was to play the part of Patton in the New York assault on Briggs and higher criticism.[27]

Chairman Birch, however, was not the only member of the Prosecution Committee who relished investigation of the Union professor. Equally ill-disposed towards Briggs were the two other clergymen on the committee, Drs. Joseph J. Lampe and Robert F. Sample.[28]

---

[25] *Ibid.*

[26] See "Secular and Religious Views on the Briggs Case," *Public Opinion*, XIV (January 7 & 14, 1893), 333-358. This survey will substantiate the thesis presented in this study that higher criticism divided the East and the Midwest. This summarization will also show that most of the secular press as well as an impressive number of religious journals were on Briggs's side.

[27] "Dr. Briggs and His Friends," *op. cit.*; "Acquittal of Dr. Briggs," New York *Tribune,* November 5, 1891.

[28] "Acquittal of Dr. Briggs," *op. cit.*; *Majority Report Recommending that the Presbytery Enter at Once Upon the Judicial Investigation of the Case*

The Charles A. Briggs Heresy Trial 93

Even more than the clerical members of the Prosecution Committee their lay colleagues revealed the mentality of the conservative block within the New York presbytery. One of these was Dr. John J. Stevenson, professor at the University of New York and elder of the Scotch Presbyterian Church.[29] Stevenson's willingness to serve on the committee showed that there were still intellectuals in the East not persuaded of the validity of recent advances in theology. But scholars like Stevenson were becoming increasingly rare.

Most representative of the intellectual caliber of those belonging to the minority was the remaining lay member, "Colonel" John J. McCook of the Fifth Avenue Presbyterian Church.[30] Affectionately known among the orthodox as the "Fighting Elder," McCook was a successful New York lawyer with big business clients. Like those whom he served, most of the laymen in the presbytery against Briggs were businessmen rather than intellectuals.[31] Warren van Norden, for instance, president of the Bank of America, was an ardent supporter of Birch's right-wing phalanx.[32] In contrast, the liberal bloc was backed by the intelligentsia.[33] Many held doctorates.[34]

Although familiar with the term higher criticism, the minority, it seems safe to say, did not possess a knowledge in depth of the new German "science." But in spite of the business-class minority's

---

(n.p., 1891), *passim,* located in the library of Union Theological Seminary; Joseph J. Lampe, *The Presbyterian Church in the United States of America against the Reverend Charles Augustus Briggs, D.D.; Argument of the Reverend J. Lampe, Member of the Prosecuting Committee* (n.p., 1891), *passim,* located at the library of Union Theological Seminary; Robert Fleming Sample, *The Higher Criticism* (n.p., 1891), *passim,* located in the library of Union Theological Seminary.

[29] "Acquittal of Dr. Briggs."
[30] *Ibid.*
[31] *Ibid.*
[32] "Is Professor Briggs a Heretic?"
[33] *Ibid.*
[34] Some of those holding doctorates were Philip Schaff, Francis Brown (Briggs's Hebrew successor), Thomas S. Hastings (president of Union Seminary), Charles H. Parkhurst (pastor of the Madison Avenue Presbyterian Church) and Henry M. Fields (editor of the New York *Evangelist*).

not being abreast of the latest theological advances, Chairman Birch and his two ministerial associates had mastered the complexities of Wellhausen's revolutionary doctrines. Birch in particular was to show in the months ahead that he could effectively hold his own in debate with anyone willing to argue the validity of biblical criticism.[35]

By the first week of April the liberal element in New York City realized that the reactionaries were in dead earnest to try Briggs if for no other reason than to guard the reputation of the presbytery against the slurs of midwestern critics.[36] So the pro-Briggs faction began to organize for another round. Once again Union Seminary, as in the Detroit attack, supplied the leadership for the defense.

Union's strategy was much like that used at Detroit. The plan was to make it appear that Birch and friends had misunderstood Briggs doctrinally.[37] Accordingly, the directorate of Union published categorical replies made by the professor attesting to his unswerving loyalty to the Westminster Confession. It was hoped that in addition to creating the impression that Birch and his committee were incompetent, the public would draw the inference that the old guard were trying to condemn an innocent man.[38]

Union's well-laid plan, however, came to nought, for two primary reasons. First, it simply was obvious that indisputable discrepancies existed between Briggs's public declaration of orthodoxy and the inaugural address. "A comparison of the questions and answers put to Briggs by the Directors and the Inaugural Address," observed one editor, "will show that the Directors of Union were out to protect their professor even if it meant misleading the public."[39] Second, Briggs himself once more pulled the rug from under the seminary's plan. Possessed of a genius for making untimely statements, he declared that he and his sympathizers wel-

---

[35] New York *Sun*, April 1, 1892.
[36] "Is Professor Briggs a Heretic?"
[37] "The Union Seminary and Dr. Briggs," unmarked and undated newspaper clipping in Hastings, Briggs Scrap Book, I, 6.
[38] *Ibid.*
[39] *Ibid.*

comed a trial. He seemed convinced that such a spectacle would provide a superb forum for both self-vindication and spotlighting higher criticism.[40]

Briggs's professed wish was shortly granted. The resolution of April 13, sparked by the minority and receiving no opposition from the liberal majority,[41] stipulated that the committee of inquiry was to begin immediately with an investigation of the inaugural address. The January 20 speech was to be meticulously compared with the Westminster Confession.[42] Birch and his committee were then to report their findings in a month to the presbytery in order to determine what action, if any, should be taken against the accused.[43]

The battle in New York over higher criticism had begun.

---

[40] "Is Professor Briggs a Heretic?"

[41] "Dr. Briggs and his Friends." The reason for no opposition from the liberal majority was that Briggs, who wanted the trial, probably told his friends not to stop Birch. See "Is Professor Briggs a Heretic?"

[42] *Ibid.*

[43] *Ibid.*

CHAPTER VIII

Why the New York Decision to Prosecute Briggs: May, 1891

One month was a short time for a committee to complete the difficult task of investigating the subtle differences between the inaugural and the Westminster Confession. The problem of time was compounded by the committee members' being heavily committed to their ordinary duties as well as to their church responsibilities.

Nonetheless, Chairman Birch prodded his colleagues into finishing the inquest by early May. He had two reasons for haste. First, the Detroit General Assembly, scheduled to convene late in May, would be attended by most of the committee members.[1] Second, Birch suspected that if the decision to try Briggs was not resolved at the May presbyterial meeting, it would have to wait until fall because of summer vacations, and by that time the initiative might have passed to Briggs and his friends.

By the first week of May the committee of inquiry had completed most of its work. As a gesture of fair play the accused was invited to appear before the committee to state his case before the group's findings were presented to the presbytery. Briggs curtly declined.

He had his reasons for declining. He actually wanted to stand trial and therefore wished to do nothing that might halt the judicial process. Further, he wished to avoid public declarations that would hamper his maneuverability as his opponents shifted their tactics.[2]

---

[1] Clipping of minutes and comments concerning the proceedings of the Detroit General Assembly (1891) in Hastings, Briggs Scrap Book, I, 22-23.

[2] "Dr. Briggs Draws Fire," New York *World,* May 8, 1891, in Hastings, *ibid.,* I, 9.

Briggs had still a more important reason for refusing to confront the committee of inquiry. He was in the midst of completing a pamphlet designed to neutralize the research of Birch and his associates. In this publication he aimed at making his position on orthodoxy so clear that the prosecution's case would appear ridiculous.[3] Here, as in previous moves, his intention was not to prove his orthodoxy but rather to prolong the theological debate. Each added day, he reasoned, meant that much more publicity for the liberal point of view.

This plan, however, miscarried, for in the midst of his writing, Briggs came down with a serious case of influenza.[4] While sick, he cast about for another way to protract matters. Realizing that he could not finish the pamphlet in time, he decided on a press statement that would review the high points he had planned to cover in it.[5]

An interview was arranged with a New York *World* reporter. If Briggs's second effort made his strategy seem plausible, his weakness for off-the-cuff remarks nullified that effort. His unguarded comments accelerated rather than slowed the work of Birch's committee.

Briggs started the interview cautiously: "I wish to say that I believe the Scriptures of the Old Testament and New Testament to be the word of God, the only infallible rule of faith and practice."[6] But after this good start, his emotion outran his prudence. Waxing eloquent, he made a number of impolitic statements which played into the hands of the reactionaries. "I do not know of one European teacher of the Old Testament," he exclaimed, "who believes in the inerrancy of the Bible. And the scholars of this country are with us as well."[7] He was even less discreet when he followed these remarks with a call to arms. Showing that even illness could not dull his single passion, he said, "We have not urged this fight,

---

[3] "In his own Defense," New York *World*, May 6, 1891, in Hastings, *ibid.*, I, 8.
[4] *Ibid.*
[5] *Ibid.*
[6] *Ibid.*
[7] *Ibid.*

although we have been ready for it for sometime. It was not considered advisable to force the fighting, but now that it is here against our will, we shall take up our arms and fight with all our energy and power."[8]

Until this press release, the committee of inquiry had not been certain that the professor should be brought to trial. His eight categorical assurances of orthodoxy seemed convincing; moreover, his silence throughout April lent credence to the belief that he had recanted. But his reckless statements to the *World* eliminated any reluctance to press charges. The committee was now certain that Briggs should be tried.

This feeling was strengthened when Dr. Shedd, now retired from Union's faculty, subjected his former colleague's remarks to a merciless criticism in an attempt to prove that Briggs entertained heretical ideas.[9]

Shedd, it will be recalled, had already prejudiced the case against Briggs in the Detroit General Assembly by a well-timed castigation. That denunciation proved ineffectual because of its superficiality. This time, however, his denunciation bore evidence of careful research. The nub of it was that Briggs "had the power of self-deception to an amazing degree."[10] This was so, argued Shedd, because the accused tried to make consistent what was patently inconsistent by asserting on one hand that the Bible was infallible and on the other that it was filled with errors.[11]

Although Shedd's tirade did prod the Birch committee to make intense research, his excoriation inadvertently served the purposes of the berated professor. When Shedd turned to the press for retaliation, he increasingly drew popular attention to the issue of higher criticism.

Capitalizing on this good fortune, Briggs kept German theology before the public by a strong rebuttal of Shedd. On the very day that the New York presbytery convened to hear the report of the committee of inquiry, the champion of eastern liberalism subjected

---
[8] *Ibid.*
[9] "Dr. Briggs Draws Fire," *ibid.*
[10] *Ibid.*
[11] *Ibid.*

Shedd to a stinging excoriation. He declared that if Shedd could blast him for inconsistencies as to the Bible and "Reason," he could blast Shedd for soft-pedaling the doctrine of redemption. He concluded with the assertion that Shedd with Machiavellian calculation had chosen this particular time to attack him in order to influence the presbytery about to pass on the inaugural address.[12]

Whether or not Briggs was correct in assessing Shedd's motive, the committee of inquiry reported that their investigation warranted a full-scale trial of the Union professor.[13] Although the decision was not unanimous,[14] the majority on the committee justified the verdict on both theological and legal grounds. Theological reasons were more prominent. First of all, Shedd's proofs were incontrovertible. Second, the committee was cognizant of Briggs's widespread influence in New York City. It was reasoned that if higher criticism's leading spokesman were eliminated, his radical movement might peter out.[15] Finally, and most important, Birch and his fellow reactionaries were certain that their investigation had revealed flagrant discrepancies between the inaugural address and the Westminster Confession.

From the angle of vision of the conservatives, it is not difficult to see why they were so sure that heresy had been found. The committee discovered the inaugural to be unsound on a number of crucial points. Contrary to the Confession, Briggs in his speech of January 20 had declared that there were three sources of divine authority—the church, reason, and the Bible.[16] Furthermore, he had clearly denied the inerrancy of the Scriptures. The committee noted that whereas the Confession clearly proclaimed that "the Old Testament in the Hebrew and the New Testament in the Greek

---

[12] "Dr. Briggs's Statement," unmarked and undated newspaper clipping in Hastings, Briggs Scrap Book, I, 12.

[13] *Report of the Committee Appointed by the Presbytery of New York at its meeting on April 13, 1891 to Consider the Inaugural Address of Reverend Charles A. Briggs in relation to the Confession of Faith,* undated pamphlet in Hastings, *ibid.,* II, 32-33.

[14] "Dr. Briggs's Statement."

[15] *Ibid.*

[16] *Report of the Committee Appointed by the Presbytery of New York . . . to Consider the Inaugural Address. . . ."*

were immediately inspired by God," Briggs's peroration flatly denied this assumption.[17]

It was this last accusation that compelled the majority of the committee to recommend that the presbytery promptly begin judicial proceedings against Briggs.[18] All signed the recommendation,[19] except one dissenter, Rev. J. H. McIlvaine, New York City minister. McIlvaine, however, was not persuasive, because his arguments were extraneous: instead of arguing from the text of the inaugural, he attempted to prove the professor's orthodoxy from other of his publications.[20]

After the majority report was accepted,[21] the next step was to appoint a committee to draw up express charges.[22] Thus the presbytery appointed the celebrated Committee of Prosecution, whose brief history would long be remembered for its medieval procedures.[23] This committee was instructed to complete its preparations by the regular fall meeting, when the trial would commence.

The formulation of the Prosecution Committee was a definite turning point in the second official assault of the Presbyterian church against Briggs. Even more germane, the decision was a major turning point in the higher criticism movement in America. Prior to the committee's establishment, the liberals had acted with restraint; the formulation of the Prosecution Committee, however, was interpreted as an all-out challenge to proponents of biblical criticism. Survival of the Wellhausen movement in America necessitated a strong counteroffensive. The responses of Briggs's sympathizers reveal that higher criticism had made an impact of considerable magnitude upon President Harrison's America.

---
[17] *Ibid.*
[18] *Ibid.*
[19] *Ibid.*
[20] *Ibid.*
[21] Unmarked and undated newspaper clipping in Hastings, Briggs Scrap Book, II, 68-69.
[22] "Professor Briggs before the Presbytery," unmarked newspaper clipping dated October 5, 1891, in Hastings, *ibid.*, II, 65-66.
[23] Philip Schaff, "Other Heresy Trials and the Briggs Case," unmarked and undated article in Hastings, *ibid.*, III, 5-6; "Hot Words on the Briggs Case," New York *Herald*, October 12, 1891, in Hastings, *ibid.*, II, 59.

The mind of most secular intellectuals as to German theology was divulged by the New York *Times*. Hitherto the *Times* had been rather indifferent to what is considered a Presbyterian squabble. But the formulation of the Prosecution Committee threw into bold relief the significance of the aims of conservative Protestantism. The attack on Dr. Briggs, complained the *Times,* in its true character was not so much an attempt to put down Briggs as an attempt by the Presbyterian church to turn the dial of theological progress backward. It was an attempt to deny the advances in biblical thought of the last fifty years, advances which had been the direct result of higher criticism.[24] The *Times* contended that the old-school Protestants had completely misread Briggs. He was not a "Destructionist." He was not out to destroy time-honored doctrines but wished to modernize them. "Probably no man among Protestants in this country today," the editorial continued, "is doing more than Professor Briggs is for the new construction of Christianity." Therefore secular intellectuals "rightly and justly sympathize with Dr. Briggs."[25]

Some notion of the convictions of intellectuals within the Presbyterian church was afforded by the reaction of Dr. Schaff to the traditionalists. Inasmuch as Schaff's response so clearly reflected the educated Presbyterian mind, his long rejoinder deserves adequate summarization.

Observing that the educated in America had been affected most by German theology,[26] Schaff accused the reactionary minority in the New York presbytery of hypocrisy. Just eighteen months before, he pointed out, the conservatives had cooperated in a resolution calling for revision of certain parts of the Westminster Confession along modern lines. Now they had turned right around and decided to try Briggs for having departed from a Confession in need of revision on the very principles espoused by the accused.[27] But

---

[24] "The Prosecution of Dr. Briggs," undated clipping from the New York *Times* in Hastings, *ibid.,* II, 62-63.

[25] *Ibid.*

[26] "Would Briggs's Conviction Split the Church?" undated clipping from the New York *Herald* in Hastings, Briggs Scrap Book, I, 50-52.

[27] *Ibid.*

The Charles A. Briggs Heresy Trial

Schaff, living up to his reputation for fairness, said that the apparent inconsistency was partly to be explained by Briggs's having expressly stated he wanted the trial in order to give higher criticism greater prominence.[28]

Refusing, however, to drop the issue of revision, Schaff noted that heresy, according to orthodox Presbyterians, was anything that conflicted with the Westminster Confession. What the traditionalists failed to realize, he argued, was that the Confession itself had been modified from time to time under the impact of rational scholarship. The Confession, therefore, does not teach the inerrancy of the Bible; all that it does teach is that the Scriptures "contain" merely the ideas, not the very words, of the divine system of doctrine. Schaff was trying to show that such an interpretation allowed considerable latitude for both the traditionalists and the evangelical higher critics. Nevertheless, he complained, the New York presbytery had attacked Briggs on the basis of the Westminster Confession.[29]

Schaff next opened fire on an even more vulnerable spot of right-wing Protestantism-biblical inspiration. "You must remember," he pointed out, "that there is a difference between inspiration and mode of inspiration." He explained that the former was certainly declared in the Bible (II Timothy 3:16), while the latter was a matter of human speculation. On the mode of inspiration, the Bible simply asserts that holy men of God spoke as they were moved by the Holy Spirit (II Peter 1:21). It does not say how they were moved, nor to what extent they were moved; it merely asserts both the divine and the human factors. It makes the Bible the work of both men and God, but it does not explain the relationship existing between the two. Thus the traditionalists' doctrine of literal inspiration is untenable; it is ridiculous in the light of both common sense and modern scholarship.[30]

Schaff next attacked the historical reasons put forth by the traditionalists to substantiate the theory of literal inspiration. You can understand such a theory, he said, only against the backdrop

---
[28] *Ibid.*
[29] *Ibid.*
[30] *Ibid.*

of the Protestant Reformation. The theory was of necessity elaborated by Luther and Calvin in order to have an absolute standard to stack up against the Catholic doctrine of the church's infallibility. A paper oracle was thus set up against the living oracle of the Vatican. However, Schaff added, the reformers themselves did not believe in what they had set up, for both Luther and Calvin held very free views on the Scriptures and had erected such an absolute doctrine only for the convenience of the people. In other words, the original Protestant reformers were subscribers to what amounted to higher criticism. Wellhausen's doctrines were therefore not new. What was new was the idea that the Bible was literally inspired, a view which, historically speaking, "has long since been discarded as theological fiction."[31] If the literal theory had not come from Protestant reformers, Schaff asked, whence had it come? The historian's reply was revealing, for it betrayed a European bias: the doctrine of verbal inspiration was "a modern American invention."[32]

Schaff's final criticism of the conservatives centered on a textual reason demonstrating the impossibility of the literal doctrine. "A literal inspiration," he insisted, "would be of no use unless God had provided at the same time for infallible transmission and preservation." He also noted that while the traditionalists conceded that the various translations were imperfect, they held the Hebrew and Greek originals to be infallible. Such a view was untenable because nobody had ever seen the originals to study them. He continued by observing that no Hebrew manuscripts existed that were older than the eighth century and no Greek manuscripts older than the fourth. Moreover, the manuscripts extant contained thousands of textual variations that presented insurmountable barriers to a belief in the theory of verbal inspiration. Not even the Pope, Schaff averred, would dare to exercise his infallibility in the area of textual

---

[31] *Ibid.*

[32] *Ibid.* Swiss-born but German-trained, Schaff never lost his love for the Germany which had so well prepared him to be one of the greatest church historians in the late nineteenth century. See Samuel M. Jackson, *et al.* (editors), *The New Schaff-Herzog Encyclopedia of Religious Knowledge*, 12 vols. (New York, 1908-1912), X, 223-225.

criticism.³³ Schaff concluded his lengthy discourse with a final fling at the traditionalists: "The Bible is a book of religion, not a book of geology, astronomy, chronology or science. To require more than this is sheer tyranny that would out-pope popery. It is enough to hold and to teach that the Bible is an infallible rule of faith and duty."³⁴

Schaff was representative of the majority of eastern Presbyterian intellectuals, as proven by the attitudes of faculty members from Auburn and Union seminaries.³⁵ Furthermore, Schaff mirrored the feelings of many Presbyterian laymen of this region.³⁶ But he knew that his point of view was shared by other Protestants. Assessing the higher criticism movement as "bigger than Briggs,"³⁷ he warned that if the orthodox clique got its way in New York City, liberal Presbyterians would be driven into other denominations demonstrating greater tolerance for liberal theology.³⁸ For Briggs, it seems, often received more encouragement from other Protestant sects than his own.³⁹

Some indication of the mind of Baptist intellectuals concerning biblical criticism was provided by Dr. William R. Harper, one of the greatest Baptist theologians of his day. A Yale graduate, Harper

---

³³ "Would Briggs's Conviction Split the Church?"

³⁴ *Ibid.*

³⁵ "Professor Briggs Still a Bone of Contention," New York *Herald*, January 24, 1892, in Hastings, Briggs Scrap Book, III, 28; Auburn Seminary, established in 1818, is in Auburn, New York. See "Theological Seminaries," Samuel M. Jackson, *et al.* (editors), *The New Schaff-Herzog Encyclopedia of Religious Knowledge*, 12 vols. (New York, 1908-1912), XI, 370-380. Also see Lefferts Loetscher, *The Broadening Church* (Philadelphia, 1954), pp. 74-82, for an excellent study of the history of Presbyterian seminaries.

³⁶ "Would Briggs's Conviction Split the Church?"

³⁷ *Ibid.*

³⁸ *Ibid.*

³⁹ The Congregationalists, Episcopalians, and Methodists were especially receptive to higher criticism. See "The Briggs Case," New York *Evening Post*, November 5, 1891, in Hastings, Briggs Scrap Book, II, 52; The Press and the Briggs Case," unmarked and undated newspaper clipping in Hastings, *ibid., II*, 49; unmarked and undated newspaper clipping in Hastings, *ibid.,* I, 2-3.

became professor of Hebrew at the Baptist Union Theological Seminary in 1880. From there he went to Yale Divinity School, where he remained until 1892, when he was named president of the recently established University of Chicago.[40]

Harper's views on Briggs's doctrines also came in response to the creation of the Prosecution Committee. While yet at Yale, he was approached by an inquiring reporter for his opinion. The gracious scholar invited the newspaperman to sit in on one of his classes for a firsthand account. The lecture of the day was entitled "The Historical Element in Prophecy and its Relation to the Divine Element."

Harper began with an endorsement of Schaff's views: verbal inspiration was nothing but theological fiction.[41] However, while Schaff argued from the vantage point of the original Protestant reformers, Harper reached the same conclusion by way of a "realistic-historical" approach to the Scriptures. He argued that there are demonstrable errors in the Bible because it was compiled with total disregard for the accepted tenets of historical scholarship.[42] "I for one," he admitted candidly, "reached the position long ago that there were discrepancies, inconsistencies, and contradictions and mistakes in the Bible."[43]

Nonetheless, Harper, like many other American higher critics of the evangelical school, devoutly upheld his belief in the Bible. "I see these errors," he remarked, "yet I accept the Bible. No man has the right to say that I cannot do this consistently. It is wrong to say that a man cannot accept the Bible and admit the existence in it of errors."[44]

This approach of the *American* higher critics, Harper insisted, had revived interest in the Old Testament, which had nearly been dead until higher criticism gave it life. Unlike the *German* higher

---

[40] Samuel M. Jackson, *et al.* (editors), *The New Schaff-Herzog Encyclopedia of Religious Knowledge,* 12 vols. (New York 1908-1912), V, 158-159.

[41] "No Power Can Stop It," undated clipping from the New York *World* in Hastings, Briggs Scrap Book, I, 56.

[42] *Ibid.*

[43] *Ibid.*

[44] *Ibid.*

critics who sought to destroy the Bible through reason, their American counterparts resorted to reason only to give the Old Testament "a greater force and broader meaning than ever before."[45]

The sentiment of non-denominational theologians relative to Wellhausen's ideas was illustrated in the reaction of Dr. Joseph H. Thayer, famous New Testament lexicographer. Professor of New Testament criticism at Harvard Divinity School, this New England scholar, like Harper, disclosed his views to a roving reporter who sat in on one of his classes.

Thayer began his lecture with the question: "What then is the correct view of the Bible?" Using, like Harper, the historical approach, he added that he believed the only way to understand the Bible was to master its historical particulars as to time, place, and person. If one accepted this premise, then the current theory of verbal inspiration was wrong and sorely in need of reconstruction. The historical approach to the Bible, Thayer argued, proved that the Holy Book was like any other document produced by men. For no less than any other piece of human literature, it showed traces of imperfection.[46]

Alluding to Briggs's coming ordeal, Thayer said the refusal to study the Bible historically was the cause of most of the Union professor's troubles. Proof that the reactionaries' position was untenable historically was evident in the fact that neither Luther, Calvin, nor any of their predecessors back to the early church held the exaggerated view of verbal inspiration. Hence there was no warrant for setting the Bible up as the infallible and ultimate appeal in all matters of belief and life.[47] Thayer, however, took his stand with the rest of the American biblical critics when he said: "But these errors do not in the least discredit the truth of Christianity itself."

---

[45] *Ibid.*

[46] "Briggs Does a Scholar's Duty," New York *World*, May 31, 1891, in Hastings, Briggs Scrap Book, I, 56-57. A good account of Thayer's life may be found in Samuel M. Jackson, *et al.* (editors), *The New Schaff-Herzog Encyclopedia of Religious Knowledge,* 12 vols. (New York, 1908-1912), XI, 314.

[47] "Briggs Does a Scholar's Duty."

The mind of the learned Congregationalists in regard to higher criticism was highlighted by Dr. George Barker Stevens of Yale Divinity School. This former Buffalo, New York, minister provided one of the most illuminating statements as to what intellectuals throughout the western world thought about the true role of German theology.[48] Stevens's convictions came in response to the query of still another curious newspaperman, who was provided a copy of a lecture soon to be given to a class at Yale.

Stevens's lecture repeated much that had been already covered by his Harvard and Union colleagues. Conceding for the familiar reasons that there were errors in the Bible, he asserted that the liberal trend in theology was in the ascendancy and that there was no stopping the modern course of events.[49]

Stevens sensed the need to clarify what inspiration meant to higher critics, for all too often biblical critics had discussed only what inspiration was not. The Congregationalist's definition of inspiration was illuminating because it accented the world-wide trend to replace absolute with relative values:

> Inspiration is a name for that guiding and enlightening influence of the Divine Spirit upon the Biblical writers which enabled them in different degrees of fullness and in varying forms to present in their writings, accounts, examples an interpretation of the divine self-revelation, such as, when taken together and rightly interpreted, constitute an adequate and authoritative guide to religious faith and conduct.[50]

Stevens's most enlightening remarks were concerned with the role of higher criticism in world history. In more precise fashion than his colleagues, he showed how biblical criticism fitted into the contemporary globe-wide intellectual revolution then under way,

---

[48] "Dr. Stevens on Inspiration," New York *World*, May 31, 1891, in Hastings, Briggs Scrap Book, I, 57. A summary of Stevens' life can be found in Samuel M. Jackson, *et al.* (editors), *The New Schaff-Herzog Encyclopedia of Religious Knowledge*, 12 vols. (New York, 1908-1912), XI, 88.

[49] "Dr. Stevens on Inspiration."

[50] *Ibid.*

The Charles A. Briggs Heresy Trial

and he illustrated how it formed an integral part of that intellectual "Watershed" later depicted by Henry Steele Commager.[51] In sum, modern theology was a phase of that process, described by Eric F. Goldman, by which the avant-garde in every discipline was developing "ideological acids capable of dissolving every link of conservatism's steel chain of ideas."[52] Present-day theology, observed Stevens, had been forced to a new method of approaching the subject. He explained by saying that instead of positing the facts in advance, the Bible was being analyzed historically and impartially in order to determine its value.[53]

Foreshadowing how higher criticism formed part of Commager's watershed configuration, Stevens explained that the German theologians had forced American divines to substitute relative for absolute standards. "The former method of Biblical scholarship was easier," he said, "since it is far simpler to ignore human factors and to define in an absolute way what the divine aim in inspiration must have been."[54] In exchange for an absolute doctrine of inspiration, one must accept a relative emphasis that modifies its conceptions and adjusts them to new facts as investigation proceeds.[55] In other words, the contents of the Bible were now to be studied by scientific methods rather than by blind faith.[56] Uniquely enough, Stevens had anticipated a truism not seen by most people until a generation later. Higher criticism was not an isolated phenomenon; it was part and parcel of a large-scale trend.

Stevens, along with Schaff, Thayer, and Harper, inadvertently confirmed another fact long suspected—that German learning had made its greatest impact upon the East. They also proved that *eastern* theological institutions were the chief purveyors of the new theology. If this explained why graduates from these schools were

---

[51] *Ibid.* Commager's thesis can be found in his *The American Mind* (New Haven, 1950), pp. 41 ff.

[52] Eric F. Goldman, *Rendezvous with Destiny,* paperback ed. (New York, 1958), p. 81.

[53] "Dr. Stevens on Inspiration."

[54] *Ibid.*

[55] *Ibid.*

[56] *Ibid.*

usually liberals, it did not answer why eastern schools were particularly tolerant of theological innovation.

Realizing that people were puzzled by this question, Briggs himself determined to provide some answers. His explanation lay not so much in regional tendencies as in institutional idiosyncracies. Why, for instance, were the divinity schools of Harvard and Yale open-minded? Briggs answered that both of these older divinity schools were connected administratively with their respective secular universities. This close relationship naturally engendered an atmosphere of cosmopolitanism, liberalism, and academic freedom.[57] Even Wellhausen's doctrines would be given a fair hearing in such an atmosphere.

Briggs next explained lucidly how the very opposite condition prevailed in mid- and far-western theological schools. Omaha, McCormick, and San Francisco seminaries were not parts of university complexes. Their isolationist characteristic had resulted from a trend that emerged after 1789. The failure of Americans to unite kindred sects before 1789 led to an era of ambitious denominationalism, with each group seeking to preserve its identity by establishing a separate theological seminary.[58] Spreading westward, this tendency produced a proliferation of religious institutions all controlled by parochial-minded sectarians. Isolated from the leavening influences that matured Harvard's and Yale's divinity schools, midwestern institutions grew more and more reactionary. Thus, while eastern schools in the nineteenth century were undergoing liberalization, midwestern institutions were becoming more and more illiberal. By the 1890s such inland schools had become insensitive to theological change. Naturally, their graduates reflected the provincialism of their professors.

Briggs next considered the one school that failed to fall into any neat category—Union Seminary. Although institutionally isolated, Union had been from its inception a bastion of liberal theology. Why?

Briggs reminded his readers that Union was located near Co-

---
[57] Charles A. Briggs, "Theological Education and its Needs," unmarked and undated article in Hastings, Briggs Scrap Book, III, 5-6.
[58] *Ibid.*

The Charles A. Briggs Heresy Trial

lumbia College and had over the years enjoyed very cordial relations with the larger institution.[59] Union's disposition therefore was in effect like Harvard's and Yale's. Columbia's benign influence on Union was as if Union were an integral part of Columbia.[60] The net result was that from its beginning in 1836, Union was characterized by intellectual independence and theological liberalism.

It was only logical that the institutional peculiarities of eastern divinity schools should greatly facilitate the spread of higher criticism in the seaboard states. Through these schools German theology was transmitted not only from Europe to America but also from seminary classrooms to the laity. Ministers graduating from these institutions often used their pulpits to liberalize their parishoners.

This development was especially noticeable in New York City and its environs. Dr. James Meeker Ludlow is a case in point. Pastor of the Munn Avenue Presbyterian Church in East Orange, New Jersey, Ludlow deliberately used his pulpit in defense of the new theology, with the consequence that many of his church members became staunch sympathizers of Briggs. This was spectacularly brought to the fore in the summer of 1891 when Dr. Patton preached one Sunday for the vacationing Ludlow. Always the opportunist, Patton capitalized on the occasion to flay higher criticism in general and Briggs in particular. The Princeton president was shocked to find the congregation in great anger by the time he had finished.[61] Ludlow's church was representative of what was going on elsewhere in the seaboard metropolitan areas.

New York City, however, was the area most intensely influ-

---

[59] *Ibid.*

[60] *Ibid.* Briggs's thesis was corroborated by the New York *Times* when it noted that Columbia and Union often exchanged professors. An instance of this was when Dr. Francis Brown, Briggs's successor in the chair of Hebrew, went to Europe in 1892 for research. The brilliant American Jewish Orientalist Richard J. H. Gottheil, Professor of Rabbinic Literature at Columbia since 1887, substituted for Brown. See New York *Times,* December 20, 1891. For a good account of Gottheil's academic achievements see Samuel M. Jackson, *et al.* (editors), *The Schaff-Herzog Encyclopedia of Religious Knowledge,* 12 vols. (New York, 1908-1912), V, 35.

[61] "Hitting Men like Dr. Briggs," unmarked and undated newspaper clipping in Hastings, Briggs Scrap Book, I, 72.

enced by Continental theology. Much of this, to be sure, was due to Briggs's leadership. But much of the work had also been done by Union Seminary. There was a very special reason why Union had made such an impact of German thought among the laity. Well known for its penchant to experiment with new educational techniques, Union initiated a program whereby lay students from nearby Columbia and New York universities could take courses ordinarily limited to ministerial candidates.[62] This unprecedented move directly exposed laymen to the complexities of Wellhausen's theories. Because of its popularity, the program was soon expanded to include professional persons who were not in school. In this fashion lawyers, physicians, and teachers were introduced to the latest theological advances.[63]

The impact of higher criticism upon New York City was intense for still another reason. Immediately after Briggs's inaugural address, liberal ministers and professors organized a secret fraternity called Chi Alpha. The sole purpose of this intellectual club was to "convert young, orthodox ministers" newly arrived in the area to liberal theology. The Chi Alpha fraternity, in short, seemed an organization to entice fledgling ministers from their orthodox moorings. Its notable success was observed by the New York *Sun,* which said that "an ever increasing number of young orthodox ministers are becoming infected" with higher criticism.[64]

To put it succinctly, New York City was a classic illustration of what was happening in every other metropolitan area in the Western world with the exception of the American hinterland. As one journal commented, the Briggs case involved more than simply the Presbyterian church in America; it was part of a world-wide intellectual crisis.[65]

The penetrating mind of Dr. Philip Schaff probably saw this development clearer than anyone else's. Schaff likened the global

---

[62] C. A. Briggs, "Theological Education and Its Needs."
[63] *Ibid.*
[64] "The Chi-Alpha Club," undated clipping from the New York *Sun,* in Hastings, Briggs Scrap Book, I, 72.
[65] "The Presbyterian Crisis," unmarked and undated newspaper clipping in Hastings, *ibid.,* I, 61-62.

higher criticism movement to a radiation process. Begun in Germany, it spread steadily westward. It first permeated the citadels of learning on the Continent, then in England, then in Scotland, whence it crossed the Atlantic to the United States and Canada.[66] Midwestern observers noted that it had even penetrated the secluded Irish Protestant church, thought to be safely isolated behind England.[67] Ohio Valley conservatives drew a parallel: if the doughty Protestants of Ireland were unable to resist heresy, would their midwestern, American brethren be up to the threat? The Cincinnati reactionaries were determined to hold the line for orthodoxy, which sense of dedication the Birch conservatives in New York found very comforting.

October 5, 1891, dawned as a day of great relief for Presbyterian reactionaries on both sides of the Alleghenies. For on this day the Prosecution Committee was to make public the charges against Dr. Briggs. The trial was scheduled to follow on November 4.[68] The Midwest was glad it had goaded the New York presbytery into action; the Big City's conservatives were reassured because they had harkened to Cincinnati. Both geographic wings of orthodox Presbyterianisms hoped that the events of the next thirty days would keep America safe from the baneful effects of Briggs and higher criticism.

[66] Schaff, "Other Heresy Trials and the Briggs Case."

[67] "The Irish and the Higher Criticism," Cincinnati *Herald and Presbyter* marked December 2, 1891, in Hastings, *ibid.*, II, 1.

[68] "All Ready for Briggs," New York *Mail and Express,* November 3, 1891.

CHAPTER IX

The Indictment Against
Professor Briggs: October, 1891

The New York conservatives had more than one reason to feel justified and encouraged concerning the action scheduled to be taken against Briggs on October 5. Professor Briggs himself had been doing certain things to help the Prosecution Committee justify its course. After returning from a summer in England, he immediately turned to public lecturing to defend the advances of German theology.[1] As usual, he made unguarded statements; some of his most intemperate remarks were made in a speech to the Massachusetts State Association of Congregationalists. A single paragraph from this inflammatory peroration, entitled "Biblical Theology and the Higher Critics," will show why the New York reactionaries felt vindicated when they read:

> Did Moses write the Pentateuch? Some say if he did not, then it wasn't inspired. Now if I know anything about Moses, he did not write the Pentateuch (Laughter). What matters it whether Moses wrote the Pentateuch? How does it affect our faith and morals? Not in the slightest degree.[2]

The Prosecution Committee found additional reasons to justify its action. Briggs also went on a poorly timed publication spree to advance the views of Wellhuasen. One of his most provocative

---
[1] Undated clipping from the *Presbyterian Faith* in Hastings, Briggs Scrap Book, I, 40-41.
[2] *Ibid.*

articles was entitled "The Theological Crisis."[3] In many respects as vexatious as the inaugural address, the article assailed not only traditional theology but the traditionalists themselves. "The trouble with the conservatives," Briggs began, "is that they have encased the Scriptures in speculative dogma." He went on to blast the die-hard Presbyterians for daring to argue that the Bible was verbally inspired. Not a single Christian creed endorsed such an inflexible position. The orthodox dogma was purely fictitious, without any binding authority whatsoever. The trouble with nineteenth-century evangelicals, said Briggs, was that they had not progressed with the times. They had rather built their premises on the primitive judgments of the second-century church.

Inviting additional hostility, Briggs next subjected the conservatives themselves to insult. He addressed himself to the question why old-guard Presbyterians so intensely disliked biblical criticism. His answer was that their motives were far less spiritual than the conservatives would have people believe:

> The real reason these men are battling us is because their kind of Bible is being attacked. Destroy their kind of Bible and you destroy them. The Dogmaticians must therefore do battle with Higher Criticism because Higher Criticism is taking away their very bread and butter. For it is destroying their proof-texts, which is the very stuff of their sermons.[4]

Because of Briggs's newest effusions, Birch and his associates not only felt justified in continuing in the face of mounting criticism, they were encouraged in their efforts by support from a bevy of influential New Yorkers. Perhaps the most prominent of these orthodox churchmen was Elliott F. Shepard, owner of the New York *Mail and Express* and son-in-law of William H. Vanderbilt.

Shepard reasoned that if Briggs could use invective, he should

---

[3] Charles A. Briggs, "The Theological Crisis," unmarked and undated article in Hastings, Briggs Scrap Book, I, between pp. 46 and 47.
[4] *Ibid.*

return in kind. Towards the end of the summer he used his paper to bludgeon the Union professor and his Bible-destroying friends. He wrote that he hoped the "whole lot of these doctors of divinity would burn in Sheol and make their journey there quickly in order to make places for a set of Godly scholars who believed in the Bible."[5] He branded all higher critics as "infidels and wicked intriguers" and dubbed Union Seminary's lawyer, Henry Day, a "retainer for the Devil." A liberal member of the seminary's board, Dr. Charles H. Parkhurst, was accused of being "abusive of Noah, Abraham and other patriarchs," while Briggs's successor, Dr. Francis Brown, was labeled "a sly and mendacious enemy of the Bible."[6]

Although the Prosecution Committee construed such printed declarations as omens of a victory, some other portents were less favorable to the opponents of higher criticism in Gotham. The New York *Times,* an accurate gauge of secular opinion, carried a stirring editorial. Observing that Birch's committee had aroused interest "not only among many persons within the Presbyterian Church but among many thousands outside it as well," the *Times* questioned the possibility of a conservative victory.[7] This newspaper's doubt was based upon the unhealthy implications of the action being taken against Briggs. The charges against him seemed to signify that no student was free to discover errors in the Bible. If he did discover any, he was either not to believe them or to keep his skepticism to himself.[8] The *Times* was shocked at the unprogressive attitude of the Prosecution Committee. "Nobody really doubts," it concluded, "that many corruptions and much errancy have been discovered in the received text of the Bible."[9]

---
[5] "Brother Shepard and the Bible," clipping from the New York *Mail and Express* dated September 20, 1891, in Hastings, Briggs Scrap Book, I, 48. For information on Shepard see Frank L. Mott, *American Journalism, A History: 1690-1960,* 3rd ed. (New York, 1962), p. 449.
[6] "Brother Shepard and the Bible."
[7] "The Indictment of Dr. Briggs," clipping from the New York *Times* dated August 23, 1891, in Hastings, Briggs Scrap Book, II, 64.
[8] *Ibid.*
[9] *Ibid.*

There were still other reasons why the Prosecution Committee began to temper its certainty with doubts. Through the summer the New York reactionaries had enjoyed the advantage over Briggs because the professor had projected a poor public image. Shepard's portrait seemed to mirror general sentiment—the Union theologian was an "infidel." But a curious New York *World* reporter was not convinced. An interview with the accused man led to a revision of his public image. Instead of a "diabolical conspirator,"[10] Briggs was "anything but the cold man that his enemies would have people believe him to be." He was a "calm man" who passed "his days and nights away in the endless world of books." Loved by his students because of his kindly "social chats before and after lecture hours," he was said to be earnest, charming, and kind.[11]

As Briggs's public image was improved the Prosecution Committee's reputation declined. Birch and his colleagues, no longer portrayed as defenders of the faith, were now portrayed as chief actors in a medieval inquisition.[12]

The Prosecution Committee was therefore glad when the calendar indicated that it was the day set for Briggs's indictment. Because the committee had worked all summer on the charges, everyone expected a long arraignment. Surprisingly, the indictment was short. Only two charges were lodged against the accused, and only one dealt directly with higher criticism. Under the one charge, however, there were seven specifications to verify the general accusation.

The crux of the Prosecution Committee's case lay in specifications 5 and 6. The first specification proscribed Briggs for being aberrant relative to the Westminster Confession on the score of verbal inspiration. This was so because Briggs had made statements "in regard to the Holy Scriptures which cannot be reconciled with the doctrine of the true and full inspiration of the Scriptures as

---

[10] "Brother Shepard and the Bible."

[11] "Dr. Briggs at Close Range," undated clipping from the New York *World* in Hastings, Briggs Scrap Book, I, 53-54.

[12] "Briggsism or Presbyterianism," clipping from the New York *Tribune* dated September 6, 1891, in Hastings, *ibid.*, I, 36-37.

the Word of God."[13] The second specification called Briggs heretical because he had "asserted that Moses is not the author of the Pentateuch and that Isaiah is not the author of the book which bears his name."[14]

Thereupon, the presbytery tersely notified Briggs to present himself on November 4, 1891, to present his defense.

It seems safe to assume that the conservatives thought they had scored a victory on October 5 because, they believed, by limiting their charges, they had an airtight case.[15] This illusion was enhanced when an effort by one of Briggs's friends to cancel the charges was frustrated. The request of Dr. George Alexander, pastor of University Place Presbyterian Church, to discharge the indictment was easily quashed by the reactionary bloc.[16]

The enemies of higher criticism actually had no grounds to justify their belief that the October 5 indictment promised victory in November. The real reason the conservative minority had no trouble in blocking Alexander's proposal was that the liberals had not showed up for the meeting. Briggs, who wanted to use the trial as a forum to publicize German theology, had urged his friends not to attend.[17]

Furthermore, reactions to the October arraignment should have forewarned the Birchites that a victory at the trial set for November 4 was unlikely. These actions are interesting not only because they measure the magnitude of pro-higher criticism sentiment but also because they reveal that many informed persons rejected the theory of literal inspiration on historical grounds.

Liberal Presbyterians in New York City spurned the orthodox point of view because sixteenth-century theologians opposed it. In

---

[13] Philip Schaff, "Other Heresy Trials and the Briggs Case," unmarked and undated article in Hastings, *ibid.*, III, 5-6.

[14] *Ibid.*

[15] "Dr. Briggs to the Bar," clipping from the New York *Sun* dated November 4, 1891 in Hastings, Briggs Scrap Book, II, 63-64.

[16] "Professor Briggs before the Presbytery," unmarked newspaper clipping dated October 5, 1891, in Hastings, *ibid.*, II, 65-66.

[17] "Would Briggs's Conviction Split the Church?" undated clipping from the New York *Herald* in Hastings, *ibid.*, I, 50-52.

a bristling article entitled "Was Calvin a Calvinist?" the New York *Evangelist* posed the question whether even John Calvin, were he living, would be on the side of the Prosecution Committee.[18] The answer was that Calvin would have stood closer to Briggs than to Birch, for the founder of Presbyterianism admitted that errors existed in the Scriptures.[19] The *Evangelist* queried in pointed fashion, "Is the Presbytery of New York City going to discipline Professor Briggs for standing in this matter of inspiration alongside Calvin, the very originator of Presbyterianism?"[20]

Catholics joined in this chorus of historical protest. The *American Ecclesiastical Review* was skeptical of the Prosecution Committee's stand because of the position of the medieval church on literal inspiration. Noting that in the fifth century St. Jerome had wrestled with the problem, the *Review* remarked that Jerome was finally forced to throw up the whole matter in despair as he asked, "For what is the use in bothering with the letter and finding fault with the errors of the writers of the chronology when it is very clearly written: 'The letter killeth but the spirit giveth life'?" The *Review* went on to observe that Jerome challenged anyone to "go carefully over all the books of the Bible and you will find so much disagreement in the years . . . that to devote one's self to questions of this sort does not appear to be the business so much of a student as a man who has nothing to do."[21]

The historical critiques leveled at the Prosecution Committee continued to come in thick and fast. The donnybrook that ensued approached the absurd when a New York City minister asked if St. Paul believed in verbal inspiration. Replying to his own question, the clergyman contended that the apostle had not endorsed it because he always placed the spirit of the law above the letter.[22]

---

[18] "Was Calvin a Calvinist?" New York *Evangelist*, October 15, 1891, in Hastings, *ibid.*, I, 61-62.

[19] *Ibid.*

[20] *Ibid.*

[21] *American Ecclesiastical Review* (Philadelphia), quoted in unmarked and undated newspaper clipping in Hastings, Briggs Scrap Book, I, 62.

[22] "To the Law and to the Testimony," New York *Evangelist*, October 22, 1891, in Hastings, *ibid.*, I, 70-71.

The most disconcerting censure was the one which called into question the framers of the Westminster Confession. The members of the Prosecution Committee were made to look ridiculous with the revelation that the chief architect of the Confession, Bishop John Lightfoot, conceded that errors existed in the Bible. "There were numerous flat contradictions in the Bible," Lightfoot asserted, "like the one in Acts 7:14 wherein Jacob went into Egypt with seventy-five people whereas in Exodus 1:15 you have them reckoned at seventy."[23] This disturbing article ended with a note of irony: "Shall we try Dr. Briggs for statements much less startling than Bishop Lightfoot's?"[24]

These historical reproofs hurt the conservatives' case badly. That this was so was shown when one pastor asked, "Where is the man who can honestly say he can swallow the Westminster Confession whole?"[25]

Other reactions to the October 5 indictment should have chilled the enthusiasm of the New York reactionaries for the coming trial. The New York *Tribune* published unfavorable sentiments from educated men drawn from every denomination in the great metropolis. The paper chided the Prosecution Committee for being so unprogressive. "Knowing as we do that every other department of human thought—philosophy, biology, astronomy, geology, history, sociology—is in the throes of revolution by rational investigation," it asked, "are we to say that there must be no advance in the domain of religion?" The *Tribune* wondered if Christian scholars were to be stopped from learning the facts of Christianity. If so, then it must be conceded that Presbyterianism was a gigantic failure.[26]

The volume and logic of these criticisms caused the Gotham moderates, who held the balance of power in the presbytery, to question the orthodox position. This frame of mind was disclosed

---

[23] "A Westminster View of Inspiration," New York *Evangelist*, October 29, 1891, in Hastings, *ibid.*, II, 2.

[24] *Ibid.*

[25] "The Real Question before the Jury," New York *Evangelist*, October 29, 1891, in Hastings, Briggs Scrap Book, I, Introduction, I-II.

[26] "The Trial of Professor Briggs," clipping from the New York *Tribune* dated November 1, 1891, in Hastings, *ibid.*, II, 48-49.

by Rev. E. P. Kipp. Although basically conservative, Kipp held that "theology should be progressive [so that it could not be likened to] a corpse buried hundreds of years ago." He wanted to know why it could not be made "a living and changing organism."[27] Kipp, as the November 4 vote would show, represented the thinking of many moderate Presbyterians in New York City.

In the end the Birch school of conservatives were supported in Gotham by only a fairly small group. The most enthusiastic backing came from Princeton and the Midwest. But neither Patton nor Cincinnati, it was painfully recognized, held any power in New York. Nonetheless, the Prosecution Committee assumed an optimistic air. Traditional theology had held sway for decades in America and had eliminated many a heretic before Briggs; there was no reason to believe that a sharp reversal of affairs was in the making.

The Prosecution Committee unfortunately failed to reckon with the facts. The Gotham liberals were determined not to let New York become another Detroit.

---

[27] "To the Law and to the Testimony."

CHAPTER X

**Briggs's Trial Before
the New York City Presbytery: November, 1891**

In many ways the trial of November 4 proved anticlimactic, for it merely confirmed the pattern now so familiar to the reader of this study. The vote and the reactions that followed the verdict demonstrated anew the division between eastern and midwestern Presbyterians over the issue of higher criticism.

The month that elapsed between the October indictment and the November trial worked in the defendant's favor. As the Prosecution Committee was continuously criticized as a medieval anachronism, German theology was given ever greater publicity.

Hence, as the doors of Scotch Church on West 14th Street were opened at 9:45 A.M. on November 4, the sanctuary was filled to capacity within fifteen minutes.[1] So great was popular interest that curious spectators were drawn not only from out of town but from many other denominations.[2] Nor were churchmen the only participants, for many business and professional men, ordinarily unconcerned with theological disputes, also attended.[3] By ten o'clock barely enough seats could be found for the Prosecution Committee and the defendant.[4] Even the galleries were filled with women anxiously awaiting the procedings.[5]

At precisely ten on the church clock, while people were still

---

[1] "The Trial of Briggs," unmarked and undated newspaper clipping from the New York *Mail and Express* in Hastings, Briggs Scrap Book, I, 46.

[2] "Professor Briggs's Victory," New York *Times*, November 5, 1891.

[3] "Acquittal of Dr. Briggs," New York *Tribune*, November 5, 1891.

[4] "Dr. Briggs to the Bar," clipping from the New York *Sun* dated November 4, 1891, in Hastings, Briggs Scrap Book, II, 63-64.

[5] *Ibid.*

coming in, Moderator John C. Bliss rapped his gavel sharply as an apprehensive hush came over the assembly. The silence was quickly broken by thunderous applause as Briggs entered to take his seat near the pulpit.[6]

Necessary preliminaries heightened the impatience of the audience. An opening prayer was hurriedly offered. The tedious roll call, which took forty-five minutes, irritated everyone. Then Moderator Bliss asked Briggs if he wished legal counsel. The accused replied in the negative, stating that he would defend himself.[7] When Bliss asked Briggs to present his case, the trial that would make history was formally opened.

Briggs's approach caught his opponents and the undecided completely off guard. Although his public image had recently improved, Briggs was still generally regarded as a ranting and reckless theologian; the Prosecution Committee hoped that he would remain in character. To the dismay of Birch and his associates, Briggs's approach was a masterly study in calmness and humility which immediately won the admiration of the fence-sitting moderates.[8] Furthermore, Briggs resolutely stuck to his script in order to avoid unguarded remarks that had hitherto cost him support. To allay his critics, he expressed ". . . deep regret and sorrow if he had in any way over the past few months disturbed the peace of the church or given pain and anxiety to his brethren in the ministry."[9]

Briggs's new approach won over some of the moderates; his brilliant defense wooed the rest. Although his remarks were shrouded in ecclesiastical legalisms, he brilliantly laced his speech at strategic intervals with subtle pleas for higher criticism. This technique baffled and angered the Prosecution Committee, for they

---

[6] "Professor Briggs's Victory."

[7] "Dr. Briggs to the Bar."

[8] "Dr. Briggs Escapes Trial," undated clipping from the New York *World* in Hastings, Briggs Scrap Book, II, 46-48.

[9] "Objections of Dr. Briggs," New York *Tribune*, November 5, 1891; see also *Response to the Charges and Specifications Submitted to the Presbytery of New York* (n.p., ca. 1891), *passim*, in the library of Union Theological Seminary.

were expecting a militant and forthright justification of Wellhausen's ideas. Briggs's clever ability to becloud the major issue was especially astute when he insisted that the two leading charges against him did not comply with the procedural rules of the church's *Book of Discipline*.[10]

For an hour and ten minutes Briggs inveighed against the legality of the October indictment. His real purpose, however, was not to prove the illegality of the proceedings against him; it was rather to soften up the presbytery with sweet reasonableness in order to make it receptive to the last twenty minutes, which was given to a stout defense of the new theology. The strategy worked.

Briggs's plan was clearly revealed as the audience listened to his stirring close—an answer to specification 6. This charge accused the defendant of denying the Mosaic authorship of the Pentateuch and the authorship by Isaiah of the book which bears his name. To this accusation Briggs replied in restrained tones:

> It is a fact that I have taught and most firmly hold and now assert that Moses is not the author of the Pentateuch, and that Isaiah is not the author of half of the book which bears his name.[11]

He then retreated into legalisms, only to re-emerge with another telling thrust:

> Even though Isaiah did not write half the book which bears his name, yet I firmly believe that holy prophets no less inspired than Isaiah wrote the greater half of the book under the guidance of the divine spirit, so that the book with different authors is as truly one of the books of the Holy Scripture, the only infallible rule of faith and practice, as if it were written by Isaiah alone.[12]

---

[10] "No Heresy Trial After All," New York *Sun*, November 5, 1891.

[11] "Dr. Briggs Scores a Victory," undated newspaper clipping from the New York *Recorder* in Hastings, Briggs Scrap Book, II, 41-43.

[12] *Ibid.* See also Response to the Charges and Specifications.

Those of the audience not lulled to sleep by Briggs's lengthy and tranquilizing introduction grasped the professor's legerdemain, for the final twenty minutes of his discourse was tantamount to an admission of heresy. Nonetheless, the assembly applauded Briggs as he finished, an acclamation "which the Moderator in vain tried to check while it continued to last for several minutes."[13]

Thenceforth, to the end of the trial, there was little doubt as to the final verdict. The only real significance of the speeches that followed Briggs's remarks was to underscore the fact that the vote would be over German theology, nothing else.

Professor John J. Stevenson of the Prosecution Committee helped make this point clear. Cutting through the defendant's maze of words, this New York University teacher said, "Under the guise of numerous legal objections to the charges, Dr. Briggs has ably succeeded in arguing the real questions at issue." Everyone knew that Stevenson meant higher criticism.[14] Colonel John J. McCook, another committee member, asserted, "Dr. Briggs's disavowal was charming, but not enough." By "not enough" he meant that Briggs had denied nothing and retracted nothing. Dr. Shedd followed McCook and put the meaning of the coming vote into clearer focus. Noting that the defendant's defense indicated no change of mind, he exclaimed, "Briggs's address could no more be squared with the Westminster Confession than you could square a circle."[15]

There were other factors which supported the argument that the topheavy vote (94–39) exonerating Briggs indicated a favorable attitude towards higher criticism. The ninety-four men who voted to acquit were preponderantly staunch religious liberals.[16] Those who voted to convict, however, seemed to cast their votes against biblical criticism rather than against the individual. Drs. George L. Shearer and John M. Stevenson, for instance, were leaders in the American Bible Tract Society, an organization whose work was based squarely on the assumption that the Bible was infallible. Hence the "tract ministry" would suffer immeasurably if the Holy

---
[13] "Dr. Briggs Scores a Victory."
[14] "No Heresy Trial After All."
[15] "Dr. Briggs Escapes Trial."
[16] "Dr. Briggs Scores a Victory"; "Acquittal of Dr. Briggs."

Writ were subjected to doubt. The San Francisco *Occident*, enjoying the advantage of geographical perspective, concluded that the landslide for Briggs was a victory for liberalism when it said that one big reason for Briggs's dismissal "was the fact that a hard core of the Presbytery's members was committed to Briggs's viewpoint."[17]

Whatever the motives behind the New York verdict, public reaction demonstrated that people thought the decision centered on the validity of the new theology.

The East, as might be expected, was happy over the outcome. Most New York City papers hailed the decision as an indication that urban Presbyterianism was not to be handcuffed by rural provincialism. Moreover, the East rejoiced that the Presbyterian church had decided to profit from the findings of advanced scholarship.[18]

The Far West, until the trial an ally of the Midwest, showed a stoic willingness to go along with the current intellectual revolution because opposition would prove futile. The San Francisco *Occident* editorialized, "There can be no question that our era of great conflict is between the new and hitherto accepted views of Scripture, with a decided advantage on the side of the new views because they are the fashion of the hour."[19]

The Midwest, however, remained adamant, with Cincinnati again emerging as the leader of the die-hards. Militant measures, argued this presbytery, were necessary to maintain the doctrinal purity of the church against eastern infidelity. Some of the measures are familiar; others had not been hitherto used.

---

[17] "The Briggs Case Not Ended," San Francisco *Occident*, dated December 2, 1891, in Hastings, Briggs Scrap Book, I, 74-75.

[18] The New York *Tribune*, November 6, 1891, hailed it as a victory for higher criticism; the New York *Herald*, November 5, 1891, called the decision a wise one; the New York *Recorder*, November 5, 1891, was glad of the Briggs victory; the New York *Times*, November 5, 1891, was happy with the skillful defense of German theology; the Philadelphia *Press*, undated clipping in Hastings, Briggs Scrap Book, II, 72, was glad that Presbyterians had decided in favor of progress.

[19] San Francisco *Occident*, November 11, 1891, in Hastings, Briggs Scrap Book, II, 57-59.

The familiar device of boycott was again put to use when the Cincinnatians once more refused to allow their ministerial candidates to enter eastern seminaries. These students were sternly "warned against teachings in theological seminaries which tend to unsettle faith in the inspiration of the Holy Scriptures."[20]

The tactic of anti-higher criticism sermons was utilized. This practice was especially common in St. Paul and Detroit. Eventually hundreds of midwestern pulpits were turned into instruments to keep the hinterland free from contamination.[21]

The most unusual expedient utilized to protect the Midwest from liberal infection was the "anti-higher criticism Sunday school curriculum." This program replaced conventional Bible stories with courses on "Evidences, Credibility and Biblical Authorship" intended to train young people to confront the modern skeptics."[22]

But the most concerted inland effort to preserve orthodoxy after the New York verdict was an appeal on the Briggs case to the next General Assembly. The Cincinnati coterie, the leaders in this drive, decided it was not enough to keep the Ohio Valley pure. The East, they determined, must also be regained for the kingdom of righteousness. The *Herald and Presbyter,* Cincinnati's Presbyterian organ for orthodoxy, accurately appraised the feelings of the region's reactionaries when it reminded the country:

> To the Prosecution Committee, the November 4 decision is a Bull Run defeat. But there were battles after Bull Run, and a complete victory to the nation at the end. So it will be in this case. If the New York Presbytery had complete jurisdiction, nothing more could be done. But the General Assembly will have the ultimate say. The New York Presbytery may inscribe on its banner: 'Let us have peace and so include in its midst

---

[20] "The Briggs Business," unmarked newspaper clipping dated December 30, 1891, in Hastings, *ibid.,* III, 2.

[21] Clipping from *Northern Presbyterian,* March 10, 1892, in Hastings, *ibid.,* III, 69-70.

[22] *Ibid.* Presbyterians in Iowa were especially prominent in this movement.

Higher Criticism.' But the motto of nine-tenths of the Presbyterians will be: 'First purity, then peace.'[23]

The immediate triumph, as the later trial of 1893 would show, belonged to the Midwest; but this verdict was to be reversed with the passage of time.

---

[23] Undated clipping from the Cincinnati *Herald and Presbyter* in Hastings, Briggs Scrap Book, II, 55; see also "The Ark is Safe," Cincinnati *Herald and Presbyter,* dated January 6, 1892, in Hastings, *Ibid.,* III, 4-5.

CHAPTER XI

Epilogue and Summary

The following two years, during which Briggs's ordeal continued, were not so fortunate for the harassed professor. The year 1892 was marked by only partial victory. The Portland (Oregon) General Assembly, upon appeal, remanded the case to the New York presbytery for retrial; thereupon the Gotham liberals again returned a verdict of acquittal. Appealed once more, the case went up to the General Assembly of 1893 held at Washington, D.C., where Briggs was suspended from the Presbyterian church. Six years later, Charles A. Briggs was ordained as a priest of the Protestant Episcopal church.[1]

Meanwhile, Union Seminary, which separated from the Presbyterian church in 1892,[2] retained Briggs and profited immeasurably for over two decades from his rich scholarship and teaching skill. To his death in 1913, Dr. Briggs published prolifically, most of his subjects being related to the field of biblical criticism.[3]

Although Briggs's inaugural address did not actually begin a new era in American theology, biblical study in this country has never been the same since that provocative discourse. Even the contemporary resurgence of theological conservatism called neo-orthodoxy has recognized the basic validity of higher criticism as

---

[1] Samuel M. Jackson, *et al.* (editors), *The New Schaff-Herzog Encyclopedia of Religious Knowledge*, 12 vols. (New York, 1908-1912), II, 270-271.
[2] Lefferts A. Loetscher, *The Broadening Church* (Philadelphia, 1954), pp. 54-55.
[3] Lefferts A. Loetscher, *et al.* (editors), *Twentieth Century Encyclopedia of Religious Knowledge*, 2 vols. (Grand Rapids, 1955), I, 180-181.

a tool in understanding the Testaments.[4] Save for a few outposts of modern fundamentalism, the rational approach to the Scriptures has become a permanent feature of seminary curricula throughout the United States.

The essential findings of this study lend themselves to brief recapitulation. First of all, higher criticism made its initial impact upon intellectuals, particularly in the East. Unlike Darwin's theory of biological evolution, which filtered down to the masses through high-school and college courses, the new German theology was long confined to the rarified cloisters of theological seminaries. Second, higher criticism in America was first accepted in eastern states. The hinterland fought a rear-guard action that was destined to eventual failure. The inland states could not be isolated from the world-wide intellectual revolution of the late nineteenth century which upset the axioms and postulates of virtually every discipline known to mankind. The death knell of the old theological order was sounded in 1925 at the Scopes trial in Dayton, Tennessee. Meanwhile, the modern approach to Protestant Christianity steadily penetrated westward, capturing all but a few bastions of fundamentalist resistance, some of which still defiantly fly their banners.

In recounting this victory for liberal theology, the story of Charles Augustus Briggs's first trial deserves recognition.

---

[4] Everett F. Harrison, *et al.* (editors), *Baker's Dictionary of Theology* (Grand Rapids, 1960), pp. 375-379.

Bibliography

MANUSCRIPTS

BRIGGS, EMILIE GRACE, compiler. Record of Letters, Manuscripts, Notebooks, Sermons and Clippings. 12 vols. N.d.

PAMPHLETS

BRIGGS, CHARLES A. *Address on the Occasion of the Inauguration as Davenport Professor of Hebrew and Cognate Languages in the Union Theological Seminary.* New York: Rogers & Sherwood Press, 1876.

BRIGGS, EMILIE GRACE. *A Sketch of Dr. Charles A. Briggs.* N.p., 1889.

LAMPE, JOSEPH J. *The Presbyterian Church in the United States of America against the Reverend Charles Augustus Briggs: Argument of the Reverend J. Lampe, a Member of the Prosecuting Committee.* N.p., 1891. (No. 7 of a volume of pamphlets on the Briggs case.)

Majority Report Recommending that the Presbytery Enter at Once Upon the Judicial Investigation of the Case. N.p., 1891. (No. 1 of a volume of pamphlets on the Briggs case.)

Response to the Charges and Specifications Submitted to the Presbytery of New York. N.p., 1891. (No. 5 of a volume of pamphlets on the Briggs case.)

SAMPLE, ROBERT F. *The Higher Criticism: An Attack on Dr. Briggs's Inaugural Address.* N.p., 1891. (No 4 of a volume of pamphlets on the Briggs case.)

The Edward Robinson Chair of Biblical Theology in the Union Theological Seminary. N.p., 1891.

Miscellaneous Material

HASTINGS, THOMAS S., compiler. Scrapbook of Articles and Pieces Bearing on the Briggs Case, Collected and Mounted by President Thomas S. Hastings, 1891-1896. 10 vols. N.d.

Scrapbook of Newspaper Clippings about the Trial of Dr. Briggs and Matters Pertaining to Union Theological Seminary, 1889-1893. 2 vols. N.d.

Newspapers

(New York City)

Mail and Express, September—November, 1891.
Evangelist, June—October, 1891.
Evening Post, October—November, 1891.
Herald, October—November, 1891.
Observer, April—May, 1891.
Recorder, November, 1891.
Times, May—November, 1891.
Tribune, May—November, 1891.
Sun, April—November, 1891.
World, May—October, 1891.

Reference Works

HARRISON, EVERETT F., et al. (editors). *Baker's Dictionary of Theology.* Grand Rapids: Baker Book House, 1960.

JACKSON, SAMUEL M., et al. (editors). *The New Schaff-Herzog Encyclopedia of Religious Knowledge,* 12 vols. New York: Funk & Wagnalls Co., 1908-1912.

LOETSCHER, LEFFERTS A., et al. (editors). *Twentieth Century Encyclopedia of Religious Knowledge.* 2 vols. Grand Rapids: Baker Book House, 1955.

MORRIS, RICHARD B. (editor). *Encyclopedia of American History* (rev. ed.). New York: Harper & Bros., 1961.

SINGER, ISADORE, et al. (editors). *The Jewish Encyclopedia,* 12 vols. New York: Funk & Wagnalls Co., 1901-1906.

GENERAL LITERATURE
Biographies and Memoirs

BRADFORD, GAMALIEL. *D. L. Moody, A Worker in Souls.* New York: George H. Doran Co., 1927.

ELY, RICHARD T. *Ground Under Our Feet.* New York: Macmillan Co., 1938.

ROSS, EDWARD A. *Seventy Years of It.* New York: D. Appleton-Century, Inc., 1936.

General Works

ADLER, SELIG. *The Isolationist Impulse: Its Twentieth Century Reaction.* New York: Abelard-Schuman, Ltd., 1957.

BOAS, FRANZ. *Anthropology and Modern Life.* New York: W. W. Norton & Co., 1928.

———. Mind of Primitive Man, New York: Macmillan Co., 1911.

BODEIN, VERNON P. *The Social Gospel of Walter Rauschenbusch.* New Haven: Yale Univ. Press, 1944.

BRIGGS, CHARLES AUGUSTUS. *The Authority of the Holy Scriptures: An Inaugural Address* (2nd ed.). New York: Charles Scribner's Sons, 1891.

BURTT, EDWIN A. *Types of Religious Philosophy* (rev. ed.). New York: Harper & Bros., 1951.

CAHILL, FRED V., JR. *Judicial Legislation.* New York: Ronald Press, 1952.

COMMAGER, HENRY STEELE. *The American Mind.* New Haven: Yale Univ. Press, 1950.

CURTI, MERLE. *The Growth of American Thought* (2nd ed.). New York: Harper & Bros., 1951.

ELY, RICHARD T. *Social Aspects of Christianity.* New York: T. Y. Crowell & Co., 1889.

GOLDMAN, ERIC F. *Rendezvous with Destiny* (paperback ed.). New York: Vintage Books, 1958.

HOFSTADTER, RICHARD. *Anti-intellectualism in American Life.* New York: Alfred A. Knopf, 1963.

———. *Social Darwinism in American Thought, 1860–1915.* Philadelphia: Univ. of Pennsylvania Press, 1944.

KONEFSKY, SAMUEL J. *The Legacy of Holmes and Brandeis.* New York: Macmillan Co., 1957.
LOETSCHER, LEFFERTS A. *The Broadening Church.* Philadelphia: Univ. of Pennsylvania Press, 1954.
MCLOUGHLIN, WILLIAM G., JR., *Modern Revivalism: Charles Grandison Finney to Billy Graham.* New York: Ronald Press, 1959.
MAY, HENRY F. *The End of American Innocence.* New York: Alfred A. Knopf, 1959.
MOTT, FRANK L. *American Journalism: A History: 1690–1900* (3rd ed.). New York: Macmillan Co., 1962.
MOWRY, GEORGE E. *The Era of Theodore Roosevelt.* New York: Harper & Bros., 1958.
RAUSCHENBUSCH, WALTER. *A Theology for the Social Gospel.* New York: Macmillan Co., 1918.
STRONG, AUGUSTUS H. *Systematic Theology.* Philadelphia: Judson Press, 1907.
SWEET, WILLIAM WARREN. *The Story of Religion in America* (3rd ed.). New York: Harper & Bros., 1950.
WARD, LESTER F. *Dynamic Sociology.* 2 vols. New York: D. Appleton & Co., 1883.
———, *Psychic Factors of Civilization.* Boston: Ginn & Co., 1906.

ARTICLES

BAILEY, KENNETH K. "Southern White Protestantism at the Turn of the Century," *American Historical Review,* LXVIII (April, 1963), 618-635.
FINE, SIDNEY. "Richard T. Ely, Forerunner of Progressivism, 1880–1901," *Mississippi Valley Historical Review,* XXXVII (March, 1951), 599-624.
LOEWENBERG, BERT J. "Controversy over Evolution in New England, 1859–1873," *New England Quarterly,* VIII (June, 1935), 232-257.
———, "Darwinism Comes to America, 1859-1900," *Mississippi Valley Historical Review,* XXVIII (December, 1941), 339-368.

POUND, ROSCOE. "Legislation as a Social Function," *American Journal of Sociology,* XVIII (May, 1913), 755-758.
SCHLESINGER, ARTHUR M. "A Critical Period in American Religion, 1875-1900," *Proceedings of Massachusetts Historical Society,* LXIV (June, 1932).
"Secular and Religious Views on the Briggs Case," *Public Opinion,* XIV (January 7 & 14, 1893), 333-358.

ARTICLES CATALOGUED IN HASTINGS, BRIGGS SCRAP BOOK
(*Volume and page indicated*)

"A Contrast: the Assemblies of 1890 and 1891," I, 4.
"A Friendly Caution," IV, 4.
"A Westminster View of Inspiration," II, 2.
Beecher, Willis J., "The Situation," I, 27-28.
"Briggs and his Professorship," I, 30.
"Briggs, Brown and Company," I, 45-46.
Briggs, Charles A., "The Theological Crisis," I, 46-47.
————, "Theological Education and its Needs," III, 5-6.
"Briggs Does a Scholar's Duty," I, 56-57.
"Briggsdoxy: The Union Seminary Should Free Itself from It," I, 44-45.
"Briggsism or Presbyterianism," I, 36-37.
"Briggs's Triumph," I, 19-20.
"Brother Shepard and the Bible," I, 48.
"Cincinnati Presbytery," III, 5.
"Clergy on the Case," I, 52-53.
"Commentary on the Briggs Case," II, inside front cover.
"Comments on the General Assembly's Action and Temper," I, 37-39.
"Defenders of Professor Briggs," I, 14.
"Directors Stand Firm," I, 29.
"Dr. Briggs and his Friends," II, 65.
"Dr. Briggs Arraigned," I, 73.
"Dr. Briggs at Close Range," I, 53-54.
"Dr. Briggs's Colleagues," I, 17.
"Dr. Briggs Escapes Trial," II, 46-48.

"Dr. Briggs Scores a Victory," II, 41-43.
"Dr. Briggs's Statement," I, 12.
"Dr. Briggs to the Bar," II, 63-64.
"Dr. Hamilton on Professor Briggs," I, 24.
"Dr. Patton: A Theological Janus," III, back cover.
"Dr. Stevens on Inspiration," I, 57.
"Doesn't Believe in Briggs, Brown and Company," I, 47.
Evans, Llewellyn J., "No Reasons," I, 21.
"Fearless of Criticism," I, 18.
"His Colleagues Defend Dr. Briggs," I, 15.
"Hitting Men like Dr. Briggs," I, 72.
"How It Looks to a Missionary," I, 14.
"How It Looks to the Alumni," I, 6.
Johnson, Herrick, "Confounding Things that Differ," I, 25-26.
"Lane Seminary," IV, 5.
"Lights and Shadows of the General Assembly," I, 23.
"No Power Can Stop It," I, 56.
"Not the Assembly's Business," I, 15-16.
"Points from Pulpit and Press," I, 54.
"Professor Briggs before the Presbytery," II, 65-66.
"Professor Briggs Still a Bone of Contention," III, 28.
"Puzzled over Dr. Briggs," I, 32.
Schaff, Philip, "Other Heresy Trials and the Briggs Case," III, 5-6.
———, "Would Briggs's Conviction Split the Church?" I, 50-52.
Shedd, William G. T., "Conjectural Criticism," I, 4.
"Should They Have Waited?" II, 9.
"Still Another Overture," III, 16.
"That Briggs Conference," I, 29.
"The Ark is Safe," III, 4-5.
"The Briggs Business," III, 2.
"The Briggs Case," II, 52.
"The Briggs Case and the Board of Education," I, 72.
"The Briggs Case Not Ended," I, 74-75.
"The Briggs Conference," I, 62-63.
"The Chi Alpha Club," I, 72.
"The Conference," I, 33.
"The Indictment of Dr. Briggs," II, 64.

"The Irish and the Higher Criticism," II, 1.
"The Orthodoxy of the Church North," III, 29-30.
"The Presbyterian Controversy," I, 22.
"The Presbyterian Crisis," I, 62.
"The Press and the Briggs Case," II, 49.
"The Prosecution of Dr. Briggs," II, 62-63.
"The Real Question before the Jury," I, Introduction, i-ii.
"The Theological Contest," I, 40.
"The Trial of Briggs," I, 46.
"The Trial of Professor Briggs," II, 48-49.
"The Union Seminary and Dr. Briggs," I, 6.
"To Sever Union Seminary," III, 19.
"To the Law and to the Testimony," I, 70-71.
"Turn Him Out," III, 15.
"Union Seminary's Loss," III, 11.
"Union Stands by Briggs," I, 32.
"Want Dr. Briggs Investigated," II, 57-59.
"Was Calvin a Calvinist?" I, 61-62.
"What Union Seminary Might Do," I, 55.
"Will Stand by Dr. Briggs," I, 29.